Praise for Tech w

"Classroom tech changed Stacey Ros[...] her students' learning to a whole new l[...] now we all can benefit. In *Tech with Heart*, Roshan takes you into her classroom, sharing both guiding principles and practical examples. With vulnerability and transparency, she shares her journey as student and teacher. The result is more than just teaching and learning differently. It's connecting and building students up differently."

—**Matt Miller**, educator, speaker and author of *Ditch That Textbook*

"Stacey Roshan uses technology to bring humanity to the classroom. In a society that focuses on speed to the detriment of deep learning, Stacey offers proof that slowing down can help us create meaningful connections and draw out the best in our learners."

—**Thomas C. Murray**, director of innovation, Future Ready Schools, best-selling author of *Learning Transformed: 8 Keys to Designing Tomorrow's Schools, Today*

"I've followed Stacey's work for years. She truly walks the walk in her own classroom and generously shares her strategies, resources and advice in a way that's applicable to all educators regardless of their comfort with tech.

"As an organization pushing schools and districts to further refine their vision for personalization, we are excited to have a book focused on humanizing the way teachers and students use technology in classrooms."

—**Shawn Rubin**, chief education officer, Highlander Institute

"This book takes a refreshing new approach to educational technology, told through deeply personal narratives about schools and education. In a world where digital tools and spaces are frequently weaponized and divisive, Roshan clearly illustrates how technology can bring humanity—and heart—into the classroom in ways that have a profound and lasting impact on students' lives."

—**Alec Couros, PhD,** professor of educational technology and media, University of Regina

"Schools are finding themselves fraught with perceived expectations of perfectionism—in both students and teachers alike. Some could argue that classrooms are becoming anxiety-ridden incubators for our most vulnerable learners. Roshan plugs into this dynamic, deftly taking the reader behind the scenes through personal anecdotes and gritty, practical methods to unlock the flame burning inside the student. *Tech with Heart* will remind the reader of their own educational path and inspire them to align with and influence young people in need of connection—to humans and thoughtful edtech."

—**Rod Berger, PsyD,** president and CEO,
MindRocket Media Group, Inc.

"Stacey brings a human element to this Wild West of school-based technology integration. There's a real strength in the vulnerability that she writes with, reminding us all that ultimately, technology should serve to facilitate connections between teachers and students, rather that isolating us further."

—**Mary Jo Madda**, creative strategy manager, Google

"I LOVE THIS BOOK! I really dig how Stacey's approach to math is student centered and focused on fast feedback and interaction, as opposed to 'getting through the whole book.' She has clear, concrete examples of how tech is used to *enhance* pedagogy, not replace it.

"I also really like how she ties stressful experiences and struggles into an empathetic approach to what her students need to be HEALTHY math students. BRAVO!!!!"

—**Jon Corippo**, CUE executive director, Apple distinguished
educator, Google certified teacher, Microsoft
innovative educator, YouTube star teacher

"As an introvert, *Tech with Heart* really resonated with me. Stacey Roshan shows us how her experiences as a student helped mold her into the teacher that her own students needed her to be. While addressing action steps that educators can take, Stacey places the emphasis where it belongs: on the relationships and sound pedagogical strategies that support the learning process."

—**Sarah Thomas, PhD,** founder, #EduMatch

"Stacey is one of the most thoughtful educators I have ever met. She is continually learning and adapting to find the most compassionate ways to challenge her students. In this book, Stacey bravely lays out her vulnerable and inspirational teacher journey, balanced with practical tips for those of us striving to teach in the way our hearts know is best."

—**Michal Eynon-Lynch**, chief educator and co-founder, Pear Deck

"I've known Stacey as an innovative leader in the educator community for several years. Time and again, she has proven herself an A+ champion of student voice and empowerment. Even with well-earned high expectations, Stacey's book amazed me. It's chock-full of innovative ideas for amplifying and engaging ALL our learners!"

—**Joey Taralson**, director of community, Microsoft

"In *Tech with Heart*, Stacey shares her journey with generosity and honesty; it's hard not to envy the lucky students who get to learn math from such an empathetic educator."

—**Stephanie Kent**, co-founder of Call Me Ishmael

"When TechSmith first met Stacey and learned of her flipped math classes, we couldn't help but feel inspired. Who wouldn't want to help share her story and inspire others to flip their classroom too? Congrats on the fantastic book. We feel honored to have played a small part in your experience."

—**Rachael Parker**, global content strategy manager, Camtasia
—**Dave McCollom**, research manager, Camtasia

Tech
with
Heart

Leveraging Technology to Empower Student Voice, Ease Anxiety, & Create Compassionate Classrooms

Stacey Roshan

Foreword by Alan November

Published by Dave Burgess Consulting, Inc.
San Diego, CA
DaveBurgessConsulting.com

Cover Art by Michael Summers, michaelsummersart.com
Editing and Interior Design by My Writers' Connection

Library of Congress Control Number: 2019934507
Paperback ISBN: 978-1-949595-28-4
Ebook ISBN: 978-1-949595-29-1

First Printing: April 2019

Dedication

To my mom, dad, and sister.

"Educating the mind without educating
the heart is no education at all."
—Aristotle

Contents

Foreword

by Alan November

Senior Partner, November Learning

This book is a special gift from Stacey to those of us who believe that learning is a lifelong adventure and that the struggle of achieving excellence is to be nurtured and celebrated. As an author, Stacey has the rare ability to share her highly successful concepts as well as her own personal story of letting go of control to empower her students to manage more of their own learning and to contribute to the learning of their classmates. While she uses various technologies to make thinking more visible for her students and to build community, she is always focused on the quality of relationships. She builds trust and a wonderful sense that learning is about taking risks and that the struggle of learning for a student is something that should be nurtured and supported. Through her work with emerging tools, Stacey is able to personalize learning for her students and to respond to the unique needs of each learner.

One of the joys of my career was to visit Stacey and meet with her students at her school outside Washington, D.C., to learn first-hand why her students are so excited about being in her class. Her students demonstrated how they use various tools and conversations with classmates to dig deeper into their understanding. Stacey believes in sparking the natural curiosity and sense of awe and wonder in every student. If you were to speak with Stacey's students, you would also know they relish the challenge of the struggle and the adventure of learning difficult content.

It has been a professional joy for me to share her ideas in my own workshops. Very often, the response from teachers is, "I can easily do that!" or, "I have never thought of that!" I have also attended her workshops at my annual summer conference since 2013. Her evaluations earn the highest rave reviews from teachers all over the world and across grade levels and subjects.

Stacey and I agree that one of the most difficult aspects of change for teachers who care deeply about their students' success is letting go of control. Yet, letting go of control is also one of the most rewarding opportunities to expand the boundaries of learning. As you read this book and are challenged by Stacey's concepts of empowering students, give yourself the opportunity to reflect on what your students would say if they were introduced to her concepts. My sense is that your students would thank you for giving them the trust and sense of safety by managing their personal risk to experience the awe and wonder of learning.

Stacey's book is an exciting adventure of "learning how to learn" for all of us. Enjoy every page!

The Quietest Voices Deserve to Be Heard

The things that make me different
are the things that make me *me*.

—A.A. Milne, *Winnie-the-Pooh*

Some of our smartest students might be our quietest. *How do we give them an opportunity to be vocal in classroom discussions without calling them out or making them feel uncomfortable?* Some of our unsung superstars may need time to think about their answer before speaking up. *How do we shift from a culture of calling on and praising the student who raises their hand first?* The truth is, some of our brightest students may feel as if they aren't measuring up because they need time to process their thoughts before responding. How can we shift from a *first is best* culture to one that sends the message that *everyone's* voice matters—and that *everyone* has the potential to excel in the classroom?

Technology has been the answer to those questions in my classroom. By embracing edtech, I have been able to ease student anxiety, bring a new level of compassion to my teaching, and get insight into my students' individual needs and strengths.

I began using technology as a means of changing my teaching practices. You see, I was that student who could never come up with an answer on the spot. I was shy and dreaded speaking up in class. I was a perfectionist who desperately wanted to please my teachers and parents and to prove myself, but so often I felt like a failure because I didn't have the answer first. My personal experiences as a student helped shape my thinking about the kind of teacher I wanted to be—and the kind of classroom environment I wanted my students to have. Along the way I have discovered that, by using edtech in my classroom, I was able to give those shy and unsure students a way to share their thinking, skills, and knowledge. More than that, the technology I incorporated into my classroom has empowered my students to change the way they think about school; they've become active participants in their own learning rather than passive consumers of information.

The story I share in this book is one that I have not seen told. My journey has not been a linear one. I invite you to join me in my struggles dealing with perfectionism, an eating disorder, a need to please others before myself, feeling inadequate in an education system that equated speed with intelligence, a career path that led me to an unhappy place, to being saved by finding my passion in teaching. I've since used my personal experiences to transform how my students learn.

Some of this book will be practical advice and "how to," but all of it will be rooted in why I've set up my classroom the way I have and flipped my lessons. My primary goal is to address my *why*— the thought process behind the tech tools I've chosen and what I am trying to achieve. What you read here will take you through my process: from rationale to implementation to evolution.

It's important to understand that my flipped classroom is not about videos at home and textbook work in class. It is about easing students' anxiety by giving them time to work through problems with their peers and with me. It is about personalizing the learning space, building relationships with students and gaining their trust, and being there to support them when they need me the most. Perhaps, above all, it is about giving students a louder voice by listening in on their conversations and customizing class discussion to their needs.

My primary goal as a teacher is to help more students feel comfortable and confident in their learning. At the same time, I want to help parents better understand how to support their children. Flipping my classroom and embracing the power of edtech tools has allowed me to achieve these goals. I'm able to check in with students on a daily basis—even with the ever-increasing demands to make courses more rigorous. My classroom continues to evolve as I more thoughtfully consider ways technology allows me to redesign lessons to give all students a chance to actively participate in their learning.

Throughout this book, you'll read about several core tech tools I have adopted to achieve these goals:

- **Pear Deck**—an interactive presentation tool. Its primary purpose: to empower every student in the room to actively engage with and contribute to class discussion using their own device.
- **Edpuzzle**—a tool that allows teachers to embed questions into videos and monitor student engagement. Its primary purpose: for students to actively engage with video lessons.

- **Flipgrid**—a video discussion platform. Its primary purpose: to allow students the time and space to formulate a response and verbalize their thought process.

Later sections of this book will cover why I've selected these tools and how I've implemented them. I will also provide ideas for structuring activities in these platforms.

01

Where It All Started

"It's impossible," said pride. "It's risky," said experience. "It's pointless," said reason. "Give it a try," whispered the heart.

—Unknown

I have my mom to thank for my love of math. She is a math teacher, and from the time I was in elementary school, she made sure I was surrounded by math. In fifth grade, my mom decided I should join the pre-algebra course she was teaching at our local community college. I fully participated in this class—taking all tests and quizzes and doing every single homework assignment. Neither of us anticipated I could have possibly done so well as a ten-year-old. It was an amazing experience. From elementary school, I went on to a Magnet math, science, and computer science middle and high school. In ninth grade, I also began volunteer tutoring in the math center at the same community college where my mom taught virtually every weekend throughout high school. I did it for no reason other than that my mom was already driving there to teach on Saturday morning, and I loved it.

Math—specifically teaching math—was where my heart was, but when I headed off to New York University for college, teaching was not my intended major. I didn't want to do exactly what my mom had done, and I wanted to earn a decent salary. My father wanted me to go to NYU's business school. I considered it, but I found the cut-throat competition among the students a real turn-off. So I went with the economics major in the school of arts and sciences (NYU offered a theory concentration, which I loved because it was all applied math) and had an incredible experience. I went on to graduate school at the University of Virginia and secured a job as an economist after graduation. I worked for a little more than a year doing cost-benefit analysis, mainly for an engineering firm that worked on transportation issues. It was a good job, but I hated sitting at a desk all day long. I knew that I needed to do something else, so I came to my senses, went with my heart, and became a math teacher.

After being in the corporate world, where individual achievement ruled, the generosity I found among other educators felt amazingly refreshing. The teachers I worked with freely shared ideas, lesson plans, and tests with one common, driving goal: giving students the best education possible. The awesome sense of community I found in the teaching world served as confirmation that I was in the right spot.

My First Year as a Teacher

As it probably seems for most educators, my first year of teaching was a whirlwind. It was also a fantastic year for me. I had embarked on a healthy challenge and my brain constantly searched for ways to improve, learn, and connect with others. I actually looked forward to going to work each day, which was a different sensation for me. Only a few months prior, I had begun to lose hope that work could ever feel exciting.

I was hired on August fifteenth. New teacher meetings started the next week, and I soaked up all the learning I could. Having never taught before, or even taken an education course in college, I understood and appreciated that I was lucky to have found a principal who was willing to take a risk on hiring me. I knew I brought strong math skills (and some computer science knowledge) to the classroom and looked forward to working with students. That year, I taught Honors Algebra 2, Advanced Topics in Math (a course for students who had finished BC Calculus the year prior), and Introduction to Programming, as well as an Algebra 1 class that I picked up mid-year when a teacher left. That might seem overwhelming, but I was in heaven. I was no stranger to hard work, so the prep load didn't intimidate me; rather, it inspired and challenged me, and helped me find that spark that I had lost.

Shifting to 'Backwards' Learning

I became a teacher to help students get a peek into the beauty I see in mathematics: to make it seem a little more fun, a little more like play. My second year of teaching, I picked up the AP Calculus AB course. It was in teaching this class that I realized I was forgetting one key factor: the almost paralyzing fear that so many AP students face at the prospect of earning anything less than an A. Being a perfectionist myself, my students' pain was all too real and left me with the vivid flashback of my own high school teachers scribbling on the board at what felt like lightning-fast speed, while I tried my very best to accurately transcribe the notes so I could go home and digest some of what we had "learned" for the day. Between trying to figure out what my teacher was trying to convey and fumbling through homework problems over the phone with my best friend, I really don't have the best memories of math class. And I *loved* math. It's always felt like a gigantic puzzle; that thrill of the concepts finally coming together and clicking was enough to keep me hooked.

So when my AP Calculus students were leaving class on a daily basis with more questions in their heads than answers in their notebooks, I knew that I had to do better. I wanted to be the teacher I had set out to be when I started. I wanted to help my students (re)discover their love of mathematics. I wanted to have time to throw ideas around and talk about math and to check in with each of my students every single day. I wanted to hear what they were struggling with and what they were breezing right through. I wanted them to have a chance to work together and to learn from one another within the school day. I wanted to make that pressure to earn straight A's a little more manageable by being there to talk them through each day—whether a bad day, a good day, or just an ordinary, regular old day.

In the summer of 2010, I attended the Building Learning Communities conference, hosted by Alan November. That conference tapped into my passion and gave me the background I needed to be the innovative teacher I am growing into today. After a week of inspiring sessions, and more exciting ideas than I could have possibly imagined, I felt both brain-fried and eager to get home to process all of my notes.

Right before I left the conference, I bumped into Dave McCollom, an education evangelist at TechSmith. As we chatted, he introduced me to Camtasia, a screen-capture tool with rich editing features that would allow me to record my screen and audio. I knew it was the solution I had been looking for to help reduce anxiety in my AP Calculus classroom.

I went home from that conference inspired and with a mission: to create a video for each of the lessons I would have taught standing at the front of the room. And that's exactly what I did. That year, I didn't do a single traditional lecture. Students watched the video for homework and then came into the classroom ready to dive into problems and discussion. Not only was the video lesson customizable to the student (with the ability to pause, rewind, and rewatch), but the classroom experience also became more personalized. Students were able to work at a pace best suited for their learning style and receive individualized help from me. What I didn't anticipate, however, is just how *little* they would actually need my help. With time and reduced anxiety, students were suddenly becoming resourceful and independent. Instead of looking at me as an answer key, they had time to ask a friend and talk things out. And I was there, constantly listening over their shoulders to guide, facilitate, and immediately catch misunderstandings. No longer was I going into the classroom with a firm agenda; instead, I was becoming a part of the students' conversations and addressing their needs for the day.

> With time and reduced anxiety, students were suddenly becoming resourceful and independent.

A few months later, after seeing the undeniable change in my classroom, I wrote a guest post for *The Daily Riff* and noted, "Particularly in AP Calculus, anxiety runs high. A rushed lesson with not enough time to answer questions and get a truly lively discussion started is far from an ideal learning environment. With the pace of the AP syllabus, easing this anxiety is a difficult task.

By eliminating class lectures, class time can be spent in an entirely different way. And this has been my goal. Using Camtasia Studio, I have the ability to run a 'backwards classroom.'"

(The term "flipped classroom" wasn't a thing yet, and my students called our classroom approach "backwards" learning.)

At the end of that year, I couldn't have been a happier teacher. My students were just as happy. My students and I were interviewed by *T.H.E. Journal,* and a quote from the article summed things up perfectly: "Julia, a seventeen-year-old junior . . . said the approach has worked for her. 'I enjoy watching the videos, and then I can go back and re-watch parts that I didn't feel okay with. Last year [in a different math class], we'd go home and do the homework. We'd have so many questions along the way, we'd end up forgetting, but they'd continue resurfacing in class. This is a different approach, but it's worked out well for me. . . . It's made math class less full of anxiety."

Mid-summer, when I received my students' AP test scores, I was amazed at the improvement. I knew I was onto something.

02

Becoming the Teacher I Always Needed

Adults constantly raise the bar on smart children, precisely because they're able to handle it. The children get overwhelmed by the tasks in front of them and gradually lose the sort of openness and sense of accomplishment they innately have. When they're treated like that, children start to crawl inside a shell and keep everything inside. It takes a lot of time and effort to get them to open up again. Kids' hearts are malleable, but once they gel, it's hard to get them back the way they were.

—Haruki Murakami, *Kafka on the Shore*

I was the perfectionist in the classroom. I never yelled out an answer unless I was certain it was correct, and I felt anxious when taking tests because it was so hard to shake off uncertainty. Even though my logic skills were in the top 5 percent for my age (I attended a Magnet High School, and the logic test was one of the requirements for admission), I hated it when teachers challenged us to learn by pure exploration; it left me feeling vulnerable when I needed to come up with answers on the spot and unsupported when I was wrong or stuck. Most of my teachers used an inquiry-based approach which, while I think there are tremendous benefits to this teaching style, was not always optimal for me. Most of my classmates were geniuses, as were my teachers, and I often felt intimidated and inadequate, even though I consistently scored among the highest in the class. I was smart and I worked hard, and my teachers constantly pushed me beyond my comfort zone. My grades were great, so all was fine, right?

All was not fine. My perfectionism made me overly critical of myself. Most of my teachers were not the type to tell a student they were doing a great job. After all, excellence was pretty much the expectation. My grades, in my eyes, could always be higher. I berated myself for any incorrect answer and felt inadequate because I couldn't memorize information like my peers or process at the speed that most of them could.

My teachers never picked up on any of my feelings of fear or inadequacy. How could they? They spent most of their time at the board lecturing and knew very little about me. To be clear, my teachers did deliver great lessons from the front of the room. Students were engaged and discipline was not an issue. They were there to feed us knowledge and to get us to think, and they did a superb job at this.

Still, something was off for me. I've only come to realize, in the past several years, that the lecture format was not what I needed as a student—or as a person. I needed to be nurtured. I needed somebody to tell me I was doing well. I needed reassurance that even though I wasn't the fastest, it was okay. I needed to know that my teachers cared about me on an emotional level. As the pressure mounted and the uncertainty around being in the same league as my peers grew, I struggled internally. I was a good kid—I didn't hate my parents, go to wild parties, drink alcohol, or do drugs. From the outside, I got through it all perfectly and always had a smile on my face.

Flipping to Address Student Anxiety

When I began teaching, I promised myself that I would bring compassion to my classroom. I wanted to let students know that I cared about them as individuals. I wanted my classroom to feel like play, and I wanted students to leave my class loving math.

I went into teaching because I wanted to share my love and appreciation for math with young minds. But I didn't want them to have the same high-stress experience that I had in high school. I don't think that my education was a healthy environment for a teenager. Yes, I was a wonderful student and learned a ton, but I was working *constantly*. When I saw high anxiety in my AP Calculus classroom, I understood how my students were feeling, and I knew I needed to do something different than the way I'd been taught— the way I'd been teaching. Lecturing had always seemed like a waste of time; however, I didn't know how to get around it until I learned about Camtasia that day at the conference.

When I began using Twitter and my blog to share about the "backwards" learning going on in my classroom, my flipped approach to teaching gained some recognition. In 2010, the term *flipped classroom* wasn't yet a buzzword. It was new and innovative. For me, it was incredibly exciting to have the opportunity to share my love on a larger scale; however, being called an "expert" made me feel uncomfortable, as did the mistaken notion that I believed *all* teachers should flip their classrooms. Yes, I think changing the traditional classroom dynamic makes a lot of sense. For me and my students in AP Calculus, this flipped model works best in our classroom. But I would never tell other teachers that they *should* be flipping their classroom. "To flip or not to flip?" is not the essential question. Do I flip? Yes. Would I recommend it? Enthusiastically, but *only if*:

1. The model addresses a need.
2. The teacher feels confident that flipping would be a solution to a problem.
3. The teacher commits to adapting the model to meet his or her students' needs.

There is no one-size-fits-all in education. Period. What works in my classroom works as well as it does because I feel, with all my heart, that it is the best thing to do. I try my very best to look at my students and to really listen to what they say. What I will share in this book are my experiences, what has worked for me and the students I work with. I encourage you to consider what might work best for your students in terms of learning, creating personal connection, and solving specific student needs. And if it's a flipped model, great!

> There is no one-size-fits-all in education. Period. What works in my classroom works as well as it does because I feel, with all my heart, that it is the best thing to do.

Looking to Technology for Answers

One key to my success as a teacher and innovator has been starting with the *why*. By identifying and addressing the problem itself, instead of looking at solutions and trying to make them fit, I have been intentional about my growth as an educator. I have been able to shift the way I design lessons to not only meet the needs of my students but to also tap into my strengths as a teacher (I have a whole section devoted to this later in the book when I talk about My Teaching Style). To get started, let's talk about why the flipped classroom has worked so well for me.

The predictable format of my flipped classroom played to my strengths (I'm a structured person who believes in routines) and empowered my students to be resourceful learners. They knew what to expect and do on a daily basis without needing prompting.

The flipped model allowed me to shift my classroom to a more participatory learning environment almost immediately. My pre-recorded lessons, which included a teacher-driven lecture, allowed my students to share their voices in my classroom. Interactive elements in my lessons, such as quizzes that I embedded into the videos that students watched at home, gave me a snapshot of individual learners' needs and allowed me to personalize our one-on-one and small group conversations in the classroom. I'd collect the data and use it to shape our time together.

In times of stress, the best thing we can do for each other is to listen with our ears and our hearts and to be assured that our questions are just as important as our answers.

—Fred Rogers

My very favorite thing about being a teacher is tapping into and gaining an understanding of what my students are going through. Being able to empathize with them is essential. As I reviewed the data from the at-home quizzes or responses after students watched the videos, I was able to see when I should tweak an explanation or probe a student's understanding. Hearing from them individually each day let me know when I needed to sit down with a student and when to give them room to explore on their own. The flipped approach freed up the time for me to concentrate on connecting with my students.

Personal Connections + Personalized Learning

I want to emphasize that last point because one of the things I value most as a teacher is building relationships with my students. They don't all walk into my classroom on the first day with a love of math. In fact, one of the biggest reasons I wanted to be a math teacher was because I wanted to change students' (and parents') "I'm just not a math person" mentality. When I looked to technology to help me solve my problem and decided to offload the lecture time to videos, it opened up a huge window of time for me to connect in an entirely different way with my students. The video they watched for homework equipped them with all the fundamentals they needed to problem-solve and have an engaging discussion in the classroom.

Shifting the teacher-directed activity to homework time and making in-class time student-driven has transformed our classroom atmosphere to a calmer, more personalized space. Outside of my classroom, sharing lessons publicly on the internet has given me a chance to amplify my voice in ways that I'd never thought possible. My videos have reached thousands, and it's hugely rewarding to hear from students I've never met when they thank me for helping them get math for the first time.

The flipped classroom has created the time and space to allow me to see how students work. I've been able to give students more "creation" tasks, like having them make their own video solutions, which gives me great insight into their needs and deepens their learning. I have been able to build in so many opportunities for reflection and peer-to-peer tutoring, and collaboration has taken on a whole new meaning. Because I flipped my classroom, class time is driven by students' needs for the day instead of content that I need to deliver. The shift in format has allowed me to connect with my students on a personal level and build the type of relationships I envisioned when I first went into teaching. It has transformed my classroom to one in which I have time to throw ideas around, talk about math concepts, and check in with each of my students every single day. "Flipping" has allowed me to create a classroom space where learning can truly thrive, where students are being prepared not only to solve the required problems but also to think and invent.

Student Satisfaction

A couple years into teaching using the flipped model, I compiled some student quotes from my course feedback forms as a way to reflect and share with others the success I was seeing. Remember that this feedback was based on the AP Calculus AB and Honors Algebra 2 classes I was teaching at the time. My students are high achievers, and anxiety is natural in AP and honors classes at my school. My primary focus, especially in the early years of flipping my classes, was to reduce the stress level for my students. An anxious classroom is not where learning—or growth—thrives.

When students were asked what they liked best about the format of class, most pointed to the differentiated, customized learning experience. They most certainly enjoyed being in control of when to "pause me." They also indicated feeling more supported in working through problems, and many remarked that they felt less stressed.

What do you like most about the format of class?

- **"In previous math classes, we had to move at the pace of the slowest kids, and that's fine, but it's nice to have the lectures under your belt and then work on problems at your own pace."**
- "The format of this class allows us to work at our own pace. **If we need to pause a video and rewind, it is much simpler than interrupting a teacher during class and asking her to repeat what she said**. I also love that we have class time to work with other students and ask individual questions. Another great aspect of this format is

that it **reduces stress** because it is so easy to make up the work at home by watching the videos."

- "The teacher is helpful, and the students are helpful, so that we can improve together."
- "I don't have to sit at home and struggle with math problems. **It takes a lot of stress out of weeknights**."
- "I loved being able to re-watch the videos as many times as I needed; **it made me feel like an independent learner**."
- "I felt that the format of class **helped reduce my homework load**."

When asked what they liked most about the video lectures, students again pointed toward the ability to customize the pace.

What do you like most about the video lectures?

- "It's nice to be able to watch the lectures at any time of day and move quickly or slowly depending on my understanding. Also, the lectures covered everything we had to know for each topic, so there were no surprises come test time."
- "The video lectures allow for a student to work at their own pace. And it is important to note that all students have different strengths. For instance, I watched some videos three times and skimmed through other ones."
- "The video lectures are great for me because I am a visual learner. It really helps me to see Ms. Roshan solve the problems and explain them step-by-step. **Taking notes on the printout also helps to keep**

me engaged in the PowerPoint and makes me feel as if I am solving the problems."

- "I can re-watch confusing sections, and it is very easy to study."

When asked what students disliked about class and what suggestion they would have for a change, many reported nothing. The fact that I consistently receive feedback from students like this suggests the model works extremely well for my set of students.

What do you dislike most about this class?

- Many students reported "nothing" here!
- "It was frustrating when we did not get enough time to work on practice problems in class and we had to go over things. I was pretty dependent on getting work done in class because I work much better in school than I do at home, and I learn best by working on problems myself rather than listening to how to do something (which is why I didn't like conventional classes)."
- "I disliked that it was only 45 minutes a day."
- "I disliked that we could not do corrections on all tests and quizzes."
- "If you fall behind because you were slacking off, it takes a lot of time to catch up."
- "The concepts were hard to grasp, and the problems were very difficult, but it was made as easy as it could've been."

I'll let the next question speak for itself. A lot of awesome feedback here.

How do you think the format of class has helped you this year?

- "It allowed me to talk more to my teacher."
- **"I think that the format of the class helped me to get more comfortable working with classmates and asking questions. I got so used to working on math problems at home, and it was nice to have the support of classmates**."
- "I can work at my own pace, with lower anxiety, due to Ms. Roshan's extreme organization."
- "Last year, it was hard to learn everything because the class was so big. This year, everything has sort of led into the next topic; **being able to work on problems in class helps get at the root of issues that I may have, rather than struggling endlessly with them at home**."
- "I was better prepared for the AP exam than in any other AP course this year."
- "The class offers **freedom and independence with learning, yet there is a large amount of support and guidance** from the teacher. Additionally, the work is well organized and is taught in an easy-to-understand way."
- "It has helped me **manage my time** and become more comfortable with learning online, which will help for college."
- "I got a lot more help with the problems in class, so I had an easier time grasping how to do questions."

- "I suffered a concussion at the beginning of the year. I missed about two months of school work. **Out of all my classes, AP calculus was the easiest to catch up on**. Also, when I finally caught up, I didn't feel at all disadvantaged from missing class."
- "With the videos, I am able to learn everything about the topic in a short amount of time and see examples of the topic. I can also understand the topic with the clear display of graphs, images, and more in the video. After the video, I am able to truly master the topic by doing textbook questions. This process works well for me, as I am comfortable with the material in a short amount of time. Also, sometimes in the past I have noticed that I may not be fully focused while in class. Since I have the videos as lessons in this setup, **I am able to learn the material whenever I am most attentive and focused**."

Finally, I asked students how they thought the format of class has *not* helped. It was interesting that one student's response for what they did not like was exactly one of my aims ... the whole independent learner bit!

How do you think the format of class has NOT helped you this year?

- "I honestly don't know how to answer this question."
- "The class helped me in almost every way."
- "I think that overall, it really just helped"
- "I don't think it has not helped me."
- **"I've become really independent, and if I didn't keep up with work, I'd be in some trouble. Luckily, I haven't**."

To summarize feedback from other parts of the survey, students indicated that they felt very supported in this class and reported overwhelmingly positive results about having an opportunity to get their questions answered during class time. All students preferred the flipped format, and none would have preferred going back to the 'normal' class format. Students felt that instruction was more individualized because they watched lectures at home. They particularly appreciated that it was easy to catch up on missed work when absent from class. Most students reported that the format of class made them less afraid of asking questions. Students agreed that it was helpful to have the video resources to re-watch in preparing for tests, though some indicated that they did not always review them often. Students also reported that they felt that the format of class helped reduce homework load (in fact, over half reported that they believed the format greatly reduced homework load), and that they felt they had more of an opportunity to learn from classmates.

There is no one-size-fits-all in education, but as teachers, we can always benefit from observing and listening to our students. Based on the feedback I've gathered from my students over the years, that's just what my flipped classroom provides: it gives students a stronger voice, it makes the classroom experience about playing with ideas rather than throwing information at them at lightning speed, it allows time to individually check in with students on a regular basis, providing the resources for them to customize pace, and it gives students the peace of mind that you as their teacher are not more than a step away when they need you most.

The Compassion of Technology

Doubt and fear always creep in. We think someone else, someone smarter than us, someone more capable, someone with more resources will solve that problem. But there isn't anyone else; there's just you. And if we're lucky, in that moment, someone steps into that doubt and fear, takes a hand and says, "Let me help you believe."
—Regina Dugan

I felt a huge sense of relief the first year I flipped my classroom. It allowed me to bring the life back into my teaching. It gave my students a voice and put them in charge of their learning. And it allowed me to individualize and personalize classroom time, making room for students to collaborate with and teach one another. In sum, using simple technology to flip my teaching approach has allowed me to create a supportive, calm, inspiring classroom. And most of all, it has given me the ability to check in with students on a personal level—hearing them talk, seeing them interact, and picking up on those small details I may have otherwise missed.

> Using simple technology to flip my teaching approach has allowed me to create a supportive, calm, inspiring classroom.

03

The Perils of Perfectionism

*Perfectionism is self-abuse
of the highest order.*

—Anne Wilson Schaef

My experiences as a student led to my deep desire to make a change in my approach to education. What I'm going to share here is intensely personal. I can count on one hand the number of people to whom I've told my real story. I'm an incredibly private person. So talking about my journey feels extremely uncomfortable, but because I've never seen a story like mine shared in a book focused on education, I know I need to share it. I believe that by sharing our experiences we can help others who may be struggling with similar circumstances. For that reason alone, I know I can't keep my story hidden. I hope that by sharing my story, I can help influence the perspective of another educator, administrator, or parent. The chance that it might inspire even one person is worth the risk to talk openly. So here it goes . . .

I developed a severe eating disorder at the age of twelve, right at the end of seventh grade. That eating disorder, anorexia nervosa, took a terrible toll on my life and health. I still struggle with its after-effects and likely always will. I won't go into the details of that disorder here, as that's not the focus of this book. But what you do need to know is that something that began when I was only twelve years old continues to affect my life and health more than twenty years later. The reason you need to know that is because school made my eating disorder worse. Much worse.

I always wanted to be the "perfect student." That desire and the competitive nature of my Magnet Middle School fed into my disorder and allowed it to take control. I was also a competitive figure skater at the time (and did ballet, modern dance, and conditioning to supplement the skating), and all those activities and pressures combined to create the perfect storm. My eating disorder was not about me thinking I was fat or having the body dysmorphia that we hear so much about. It was about control and being perfect in environments that I didn't always know how to properly navigate.

When I transitioned from my neighborhood elementary school to a Magnet Middle School, I left all my friends and had to start from scratch. The new school's environment was incredibly competitive. During the first couple of weeks at school, I felt so unnerved by everything being so new and confusing that I had no appetite at lunch. I remember buying only a small bag of Smartfood Popcorn for lunch on the first day, and not even being able to finish that. I wasn't trying to restrict calories in any way, I just wasn't hungry. I didn't think much of it at the time, but the fact that I was able to barely eat all day that first day of school was an empowering snapshot in my mind by the end of that same school year.

I did well in middle school from the start. But it wasn't easy. School was never easy because I always needed to go that extra mile. I was pretty darn smart and had made it into the Magnet program where I earned just about straight A's. But I worked my butt off. I never knew "good enough." I could always do better, and I always pushed myself harder. There was such competition all around me—from my peers, from their parents, and from my own parents.

In the classroom, I was excited to contribute but felt too shy to raise my hand. It wasn't always easy to verbalize what was in my head when I was called on. I was never quick. Even when I was in elementary school, I vividly remember being so slow when we did multiplication and division flashcards. I had a really hard time with those facts and often had to count on my fingers. I would hide my fingers under the table because we weren't allowed to use our fingers to count. Naturally, I thought I wasn't as good at basic arithmetic as my peers (even though, when we did the complex long division problems where everyone was struggling, I was able to do the most challenging problems assigned).

Math was always my favorite subject, and I loved my middle school Algebra teacher. She was tough and very strict, but I did well in the class and learned so much. I credit her for helping solidify my love of math and growing my reasoning ability to a high level early on. One of the biggest problems with the class structure for me, though, was that we had daily warm-up quizzes on recalling the various theorems verbatim. We were docked points for incorrect spelling or even a word out of place. As luck would have it, my algebra class just happened to fall right after lunch in my schedule, which meant that each day at lunch, I would test myself and worry about the quiz next period. It's probably not surprising to read that these concerns affected my appetite and ability to eat my lunch.

Slow Isn't the Opposite of Smart

Thanks to Stanford Professor and Founder of YouCubed Jo Boaler, the long-held stigma about kids (or adults!) using their fingers to count is finally changing. Check out her article in The Atlantic titled "Why Kids Should Use Their Fingers in Math Class." Researchers at Stanford also stress that some students simply learn better by using visual tools than by memorizing the multiplication tables and reciting them as quickly as possible. "When I introduce math problems to my Stanford students, I say, 'I don't care about speed; in fact, I am unimpressed by those who finish quickly. That shows you are not thinking deeply,'" says Boaler. "Instead, I would like to see interesting and creative representations of ideas."

All Eating Disorders Are Not Created Equally

Like so many other factors, habitually skipping lunch when I was stressed or worried contributed to my restrictive eating pattern spiraling out of control. It wasn't one single thing that led to my eating disorder; there were a lot of little things. I felt like I wasn't quick enough. My class environments felt so highly competitive that I didn't feel "safe." The biggest problem spots in my personality were (and still are) my perfectionism and strong desire to be in control. In middle school, I started feeling a greater need to tighten my grip on those two things. I found the safety and sense of control I craved by controlling what I ate. And the anorexia crept in.

My eating disorder revolved around control. It wasn't about getting super skinny. As I lost weight, I could see that I looked like a skeleton, and I hated my appearance. Prior to developing anorexia, I had always been an athletic kid, muscular and strong. From all the training, my legs were toned and built to land jumps. Remember, I was a competitive figure skater up until I was in tenth grade. Somewhere along the way, however, I determined that I wanted perfect control over the number of calories that entered my body. It became a game of seeing the number on the scale go down (even if I was terrified of losing any more weight). None of it was rational, but having control over those numbers—when I felt I had so little control over the external world—made me feel better.

My eating disorder somehow empowered me, or, rather, it tricked me into feeling empowered. When I restricted my food, I felt like I had laser focus on my school work. When my stress was high, my stomach would hurt and make me feel sick, which kicked off a vicious cycle of eating even less. The less I ate, the lighter I got, and the more powerful I felt.

I wish I could tell you a simple story of getting help and recovering from anorexia. I never did go into in-patient treatment. And I've had a lot of terrible experiences trying therapy and feeling very misunderstood. The truth is that I relapsed hard when I went to college. Though I was severely undernourished, yet again I thrived in my studies. There is no logic in this. And it perpetuated the cycle. My final full-blown relapse was when I was working as an economist. That was my lowest and scariest point, and it took its toll on my body. As a muscle that isn't used atrophies, my ability to digest food properly deteriorated. After years and years of working with doctors, I still struggle with digestive problems and other health concerns. A body can only take so much.

What saved me was finding a naturopathic doctor with a truly holistic approach. Dr. Charlene Kannankeril has helped me identify foods that work for me and supplements to relieve some of my symptoms. Though I don't want to focus too much time and energy in this book on my eating disorder, I have to tell you that traditional eating disorder therapy didn't work for me. In fact, it made me much worse. With the help of Dr. Kannankeril, I have learned to regiment my food and follow an eating plan, which has allowed me to get to the best place I've ever been in my life. I am no longer scared of food in the way I once was. What I have not overcome is the extreme shame I feel in the structured way that I eat, even though I know this works for me and keeps me healthy. I usually hide from this truth, so it shocks me that I am writing it here. Perhaps I need to share to move forward?

> *My entire life changed because discipline allowed me to be in control again. I was no longer scared because I knew that discipline could rescue me from the deepest, darkest place.*
> —Tim Denning

Yet again, this story is one in which a one-size-fits-all approach did not work for me—and another reason that I so strongly believe in treating each child in my classroom as an individual, doing the best to listen to their whole story.

Perfectionism still plagues me at times, and those fears that surface help me to be aware of how lost and insecure so many of our students feel—even if they're earning high marks. It is my greatest hope that reading this book will help you spot those feelings, too.

Teaching with Heart

My experiences with perfectionism and anorexia have had a profound impact on how I choose to run my classroom. As a teacher, I try my hardest to be an observant listener. I don't ever assume that I can know what a student is going through. I know that I will not always be able to pick up on what might be troubling a student internally. Perhaps nobody could have saved me from the deep, dark mess of a road that I went down. But maybe one of my teachers could have observed something along the way if the classroom dynamic had been different—if teachers had more time to sit with me, if I had more opportunities to chat things out with them instead of watching them spend the majority of class time on the board at the front of the room, if I could have had a different definition of what it meant to be the "perfect student." Those "what if" questions I ask myself have shaped the way I teach. They are my *why* for sharing my teaching approach on social media and at conferences, and it's why I'm sharing my story with you now. I know that we can make a difference in our students' lives—yes, of course, academically but also, and more importantly, in the way they perceive themselves as humans.

Rewinding back to my 2009 AP Calculus class, when the bell rang each day, I felt like we all had just stepped off a giant treadmill after running full speed for forty-five minutes. I had so much material to get through and a very anxious class; there simply wasn't enough time to have a calm, excited, inspiring classroom atmosphere. Worst of all, I barely got to hear from students because they were focused on digesting new material. We didn't have time for the lively, thoughtful discussion that's necessary for developing higher-logic thinking (not to mention where the real fun and secret learning happens).

Compassion is a huge focus for me as a teacher. In assessing the optimal dynamics for my classroom, I continually ask myself the following questions:

- What activities are students gaining the most from?
- What valuable activities am I not making enough time for?

- What could we do without?
- How can I create more time to talk with and get to know my students?
- What am I most excited and passionate about?

As I thought about the answers to those questions back in the summer of 2010, I also considered the reality that school (and math in particular) often follows a boring, rigid learning environment where the teacher lectures and the students practice until the skill is mastered. My solution for creating time to do things that mattered was to eliminate lecture. When I learned about Camtasia, I immediately knew I had the power to completely change my classroom, and I haven't lectured new material in AP Calculus since.

In the first year I flipped, the mean AP score for my class went up over half a point (on a five-point scale) from our highest recorded average in previous years. Since that time, students have continued to thrive academically in the flipped environment. But more than that, my students seem so much happier and alive since I made a shift to my teaching style.

Some people argue that using technology in education feels automated and less personal. I've found the exact opposite to be true. Using technology has brought the compassion back into my classroom. Beyond the improved test grades and AP scores, the differentiated and customized learning experience the flipped classroom provides, the lasting resources I have given my students to reference throughout the year (and beyond), and the significant improvement in performance I have seen in

> Some people argue that using technology in education feels automated and less personal. I've found the exact opposite to be true.

some of my students with learning accommodations, the flipped classroom has allowed me to create a supportive and positive environment. I'm there to listen, to support, and to hear all the chatter that's going on around the room. That, to me, is the greatest benefit of all!

Tech with Heart

STRESS

Impossible Homework   Math Anxiety

Need Real-Time Help

Not enough TIME to indiwalize
& customize

30

04

Flipping for the First Time

I have high expectations for you, and I know you can meet them. So try this new challenge and if you fail, I'll help you recover.

—Chip Heath and Dan Heath,
The Power of Moments

Clearly, I wholeheartedly believe in the benefits of the flipped classroom model, and I know that there is no one-size-fits-all approach to teaching. After almost ten years using and adapting this model to meet the needs of the students in my classroom, I am convinced that not only has it empowered my students to learn more effectively, but it has also enabled me to be the kind of teacher I want to be. For me, the flipped classroom is all about shifting my classroom environment to one that is centered around students' needs versus content that I need to deliver. We still cover the content, but this model simultaneously provides avenues to build strong relationships with my students and individualize instruction. Using video lessons means that students can rewind and review and take in information at the speed that is most comfortable for them. And because they work collaboratively in the classroom to solve problems, the stress of homework is greatly reduced. Having established the rationale, in this chapter we'll begin to explore the *how* of flipping the classroom—beginning with how to get others on board with the idea.

Shifting the (Math) Class Mindset

I recently saw this quote from digital analyst and founder of FutureWorks Brian Solis: "Technology is often the right thing to 'do' but the 'why' it's introduced with is often the missing ingredient to success. Technology alone, though, isn't the answer."

I couldn't agree more strongly.

With that reality in mind, I've worked hard to shift the mindset of what school can look like—and specifically what math class can look like. Traditional math classes can fill some students with stress and anxiety. Often, it's those emotions that make the subject a turnoff. The heavily lecture-based classes leave little time for classroom practice or discussion, so solving problems happens at home in isolation. When the homework feels too overwhelming to start or impossible to complete, student (and parent) anxiety levels rise. Students may feel as if they don't have the help they need to complete their work—or to simply understand the content— which adds to the stress and undermines their ability to reach their full potential.

In a classroom where most of the teacher's time is spent at the board lecturing to the needs of the classroom as a whole, especially with the packed curriculum of an AP course, there is not enough time to customize on a personal level. One of my biggest goals as a teacher is to provide a safe environment for all students, where they can get their questions answered and work at a pace that best fits their needs. I want to be there for my students when they need me and to get to know them as individuals. I work to push my students beyond their comfort zones, all the while ensuring that the supports are in place should they need help.

During a traditional math lecture, you might see students scribbling notes verbatim from the board and, although they are paying close attention, they are not fully engaging and participating in the learning process. For many, that's because the information is coming at the wrong pace—either too fast and they can't keep up or too slow and their mind wanders to other things.

In my classroom, we have reversed the traditional format. We do problem-solving in the classroom. Discussions, driven by student needs and concerns, take place in class where we can work on the problems at the board or in groups. Then, for homework, students watch a video lesson which equips them with the fundamentals they need to have engaging discussions the next day. As they watch, they take notes on a handout, which then serves as the starting point for our in-class discussion.

In addition to having their handout to complete, I build interactivity and monitoring into the videos. Embedded quizzes serve as learning checks and provide instant feedback to the student. On-the-spot correction can be critical in helping students identify areas where further review is needed and helps prevent bad habits and misconceptions. The quizzes in the video are never graded; they are only meant to help both me and the student identify areas where more explanation or focus is needed. In addition, callout boxes, highlights, and pointers in the video help draw attention to important elements, and the video will pause for emphasis to draw attention to main points.

Putting students in the driver's seat is also an important part of my classroom. In creating video lectures myself and posting them online, I have been able to experience the wonder of having my voice reach far beyond my immediate classroom. Students around the world turn to YouTube or an internet search when they are looking to learn something new. Students in my classroom are asked to contribute in a similar way. They have opportunities to create and share mini video lessons of their own. They also contribute to online math communities, answering and asking questions. Creating videos and participating in online discussions requires them to be able to verbalize their learning and explain their solutions, which helps solidify concepts and deepen their understanding.

For the teacher, the parent, and the student, it is essential to develop the proper mindset about the flipped classroom model from the onset. When the teacher-directed learning happens at home, the classroom can become more student centered and student driven. The classroom space can then be supportive, calm, and inspiring. Students are given ample time to do collaborative problem-solving. When parents understand that the flipped classroom is all about giving students more ownership of their learning, and that the teacher is there to guide students, listen to questions, and support them, they will be more excited about your approach. If you're flipping a class for the first time, your students and parents may have some reservations. That's where good communication and strong relationships come into play.

Good Communication with Parents Is Essential

When I began flipping my AP Calculus AB classes, I received very few questions from parents. The reason for that, I think, was 1) parents tend to be a bit more hands-off with juniors/seniors, and

2) the students' previous math class had been challenging enough for parents to feel lost on homework assignments at times. When I flipped AP Calculus AB, my students were actually excited about being able to do work on the problems in the classroom, where they had my support as well as help from their peers. The parents were happy because the students excelled with the new class format. All in all, year one in that class went extremely smoothly.

I cannot say the same about the first month of Honors Algebra 2. By the end of the year, things were absolutely awesome, but it took a couple of months at the beginning of the year—and a lot of time and effort on my part—to get everyone on board. From that not-so-great experience, I learned a lot about the importance of communication and building relationships with parents.

Building trust with parents can be critical to your students' success in any class, but because a flipped approach is not the norm, explaining the process and the why behind it is essential. In my experience, parents just want to know that their child is going to be in a class where the teacher genuinely cares about their son/daughter as an individual. With that in mind, the best advice I can give you is to be clear about your expectations with students and their parents and intentional about building meaningful, strong relationships—starting with back-to-school night.

Many teachers dread back-to-school night. It's a fast-paced, hectic evening. Throughout the years, however, I've learned that this is where the relationship building begins. Back-to-school nights provide an opportunity for me to share my passion for what I do. I have the chance to talk face-to-face with parents, to outline my expectations, and to talk about how I am going to help their son/daughter grow academically and personally.

Explaining the flipped classroom to parents in the extremely brief amount of time I have on back-to-school night is a challenge. And that is where I went wrong the first year when I flipped

Honors Algebra 2. I gave an overview of the model, but parents left confused.

One of the most eye-opening conversations I had that year was with the parents of a student who was struggling and very anti-flip. During the conversation, one of the parents actually said, "I just didn't understand what you were saying at back-to-school night. There was so much information being given out, I just couldn't process it all." In that moment, they had articulated the *why* behind flipping the class. When I explained my purpose, our conversation—which had started with frustration on their part because their son was unhappy—ended with them thanking me and saying they were going to have a conversation with their son to help him understand my expectations, as his teacher, and their expectations, as his parents. Understanding the why behind the flipped model transformed everything for them. With their encouragement, the student started taking responsibility for his learning, earned A's and high B's all year, and ended up loving the class. He even selected me to be his advisor after that and continued to stop by my classroom at least twice a week to just say hi.

To avoid similar frustration and confusion the next year, I knew that I needed to efficiently explain what my flipped classroom was all about and the motivation behind reversing the traditional classroom dynamic. I also knew it had to be an engaging presentation, because those parents I had conferenced with the year prior had been right; back-to-school night is information overload, particularly after a long day of work. The solution: I made a video! Genius, right? This time, I used VideoScribe to create an engaging presentation that addressed my motivation for flipping the classroom, explained what classwork and homework would look like, and described how I hold students accountable for doing their work. I then closed by emphasizing what the flipped classroom means to me. Since I didn't want to give parents pre-work, we all watched this video together in the first couple minutes of back-to-school night. After the video, I went through my I went through my expectations, class webpage, and calendar, and then then I had time for questions at the end. I then posted the video for parents to review if they needed to watch again—and also for those parents who were unable to attend back-to-school night. Clear communication is key, and for me, making this video made a huge difference!

SO WHAT'S REALLY FLIPPED ABOUT THE FLIPPED CLASSROOM?

Role of student -
resourceful & independent
responsible & helpful

Classroom climate -
collaborative and supportive
mistakes are part of the learning process

My role -
facilitator & guide

Listening to questions & joining THEIR discussions

Check out the video at bit.ly/flipclasswelcome

Course Development—Start with Your Why

When I first flipped my class—and any time I make changes to my courses—I considered these essential questions:

- How can I address each student's questions and concerns to ensure comprehension?
- How can I make sure I have enough time to connect with every one of my students on a personal level?

- How can I make sure learning remains enjoyable and is not outweighed by the stress of increasingly high academic demands?
- How can I provide a differentiated learning environment where all of my students feel safe in responding?
- How can I give each student in the classroom an equal voice?

As an example, here is the thought process behind my decision for students to have a weekly student-led video chat requirement in my Online AP Calculus AB course. I will talk in more detail about my purely online section of AP Calculus AB. But for now, I will just include the fact that this is a course offered to tenth through twelfth graders at my school who want to experience a fully online class or who have a scheduling conflict. The basic structure of the class is that students:

1. Watch a daily video lecture and complete "quiz" questions I've embedded through Edpuzzle.
2. Work a series of problems, scan their handwritten solutions via phone app, and submit.
3. Participate in one full-class, synchronous Zoom session per week (teacher-led).
4. Lead a small-group Zoom session per week with 2-3 classmates (student-led).

As with my in-person courses, collaboration is an important part of learning. My goal was to make sure students understood that our online class format was not about working in isolation. There is tremendous power in problem-solving with others and working through challenges with classmates. This is something I value most about the format of my flipped classroom. Helping peers is an important component of my math courses, but creating opportunities for group work needed to make sense and not simply be about creating extra work or busy work for my students.

My solution was for students in my purely online section to record small group video chats. Initially, I wasn't sure how this would go. Would students know what to talk about? Would they take it as seriously as class time? Would I need to provide strict guidelines for what they should do? In the first two weeks of class, I was able to model expectations when I led our full class synchronous Zoom session. By the third week of class, students were expected to lead their own small group Zoom. The only real instruction I gave them beyond teaching the technical parts of setting up, recording, and submitting their Zoom session was to use the time to get work done collaboratively! Students picked up on my model naturally, and they didn't need much intervention beyond that from me.

For each group chat submitted, I review the entire video and leave feedback to clarify any questions asked, as well as correct any mistakes I hear students chatting about. Though reviewing this assignment is time-consuming, it is one of the most valuable components of class in terms of intimately getting to know students' needs. I learn so much from listening to the students' voices, hearing where they speak fluently versus areas marked by uncertainty and hesitation. When I play back this recording, I get to hear my students work through problems as they help one another, I get to view their interactions with classmates, and I get a feel for how they're approaching problems. Working together and peer-to-peer learning is the name of the game in this activity! Discussion boards and instant messaging are awesome, but there is something about hearing my students talk that really helps me feel more connected to them as individuals. Seeing them chat about math, casually in this manner, helps me feel connected with my online students— and it helps them connect and learn with one another.

Honestly, I have been absolutely amazed by how much good work gets done by students in these thirty-minute chats. The activity is entirely student-led, and they are responsible for setting up their own guidelines for what they plan to accomplish during the hangout. Students are held accountable for responsibly organizing the session because they know they will need to submit the video link to me, and they know that I am going to take the time to watch their recording in its entirety and leave helpful feedback. They also know that the best feedback comes when they ask good questions.

Collaboration is such an important component of my course design. Meeting that need for working together—whether it's in a traditional classroom setting or in an online course—is definitely one of the *whys* I work to address. My students know they are never working alone, even those who are taking an online class. In my classroom, we hold discussion at the board or work together in small groups. In my Online AP Calculus AB class, we are constantly chatting and interacting in the class Slack channel.[1] When I see that a student needs help, I can work with him one-on-one in class; or if it's in my online course, I can send a direct message through Slack and leave a short video for clarification. Regardless of the class format, I work to keep my *why* of collaboration as a key element of the course.

As you consider your own class goals, think about your *why*. What do you want to make more time for in class? What can you eliminate? What would help your students collaborate and learn more effectively? Those are your whys. Start there.

---

1 To create a strong sense of community in the course, we use Slack for real-time messaging and chat. (I discuss this more in Chapter 7.) I want to note that all my students are over sixteen, which is why we can use this platform. Per Slack's terms of service, all users must be over the age of sixteen years of age to use.

Flipped Classroom Timeline

Making a major change to your teaching practice doesn't happen overnight. That was true for me when I started flipping my classroom. I want to give you a brief overview of how my classroom has evolved over time. In later chapters, I'll go into more detail about the specific tools and techniques mentioned, but I want you to see that shifting to a flipped model can be a gradual process that improves as you learn what works and what you want to see more of in your classroom.

Year One

Using Camtasia, a tablet PC, and PowerPoint, I focused on making the videos for each lesson in year one. It still takes me hours to create each video, but I care a lot about the quality of my content, so I take the time to craft a lesson that can be absorbed in video form, add appropriate visuals to aid in comprehension, and edit out any misspeaks. Some people can make a video in one take without needing to edit. That's never been the case for me. So the first year I flipped my class, I focused only on creating the video lessons.

Year Two

My second year, I reused the videos I had created and took more time to think about what we were doing in the classroom. This involved thinking about what questions I was going to ask at the start of class to really force students to take their learning to a deeper level. I structure my video lessons to equip students with the building blocks and necessary vocabulary for each day's lesson. Then, in class, we break down the lesson to allow higher-order discussion and thinking to take place. It's important that I prompt my students with the right questions to really help them develop strong logic and reasoning skills.

This discussion time is an essential part of a successful flipped classroom. As I became aware that the same few students were the ones to raise their hands or contribute to the discussion, I began looking for a way to give every student an opportunity to respond in a way that was optimal for him or her. (I could have just called on students at random, but based on my personal story, I bet you can guess that I dismissed that option right away.) I didn't find the solution to this problem in year two, but I kept it on the top of my list of goals.

Year Three

In year three, I decided to implement the flipped model in my Honors Algebra 2 classes. This is also when I discovered Pear Deck, an interactive presentation tool that allows all students to engage with questions from their own device. Two major things happened in this year:

1. I embedded quizzes into all of my Honors Algebra 2 videos directly through the Camtasia editor.
2. I began using Pear Deck for warm up as a way to give all students an opportunity to "speak."

Year Four

In year four, it was time to focus my energy back on my AP Calculus AB course and embed quizzes into each of those videos. I also refined and re-recorded a bunch of videos as I found sections to improve. I worked on ways for students to have more opportunities to create by having them screencast solutions on an iPad and upload that to a class YouTube channel.

Year Five

In year five, I moved all embedded quizzing and video interactivity over to Zaption, which was a platform specifically targeted at making videos interactive. I made the switch because the analytics Zaption provided were more robust than what I was receiving through Camtasia. As I started seeing the power of adding interactive elements and quizzing into my videos, I knew I needed to prioritize transitioning to the platform that could provide the best level of feedback to meet the needs of my students. I talk, in depth, about how Zaption transformed my teaching in Chapter Six.

That year, I also focused on having students verbalize their math and contribute to a global community of math learners. I began having students post to Socratic.org, a question-and-answer site for academic subjects, on a regular basis. Each unit, I would assign students one or two questions to answer (additional response posts would show an individual interest beyond class requirements and reflect the student's effort to go above and beyond). Socratic is a global forum, and students can actually see, on a map, the impact of their post. Additionally, in creating a typed solution, students are required to break down difficult concepts in words and write out their thought process in detail. These posts became a resource for the class to study from, and we have since built a large library of student-created answers that I use in my instruction.

Year Six

In year six, I focused on using Pear Deck even more effectively. I created better questions to help students discover and make connections between topics. With our class set of Wacom tablets, we used Pear Deck regularly to solve warm-up problems. The responses from Pear Deck served as the basis to kickstart our class discussion.

Year Seven

In year seven, I started teaching Online AP Calculus AB. I wanted to create a strong class community, so I looked to new tools, including Zoom and Slack, which allowed conversations to happen anytime, anyplace. The result was that students felt supported online as well as in our classroom. I also started using Flipgrid in creative ways to help my students talk out their solutions and give valuable insight into their processes and approaches.

Year Eight

In year eight, I focused on making student reflection a more intentional activity and part of our class routine. Flipgrid and Zoom continued to be valuable tools in making strong connections with my students. I also started using Sutori, a timeline tool, to ask students to document growth and make connections between the old and the new. I explain this assignment fully in Chapter Nine.

My Teaching Style

One more thing to consider before you begin to flip your classroom is your teaching style. My personality and style have made me a much better and more successful teacher by flipping the classroom dynamic. Here is how I see it …

I'm a planner. I like having an agenda, I like knowing what my day will look like, I like being prepared. Being spontaneous definitely takes me out of my comfort zone. I am an introvert, and there is no question about it. I am the opposite of a procrastinator and like working a little too far ahead. I am a perfectionist to a fault, and this is something I am working on. I am addicted to learning, I'm constantly reading, and I love taking things apart and putting them together without reading instructions.

Teaching pushes me in ways that I need to be pushed, while allowing me to work within my strengths zone. I always walk into the classroom with an agenda, but the classroom requires enormous flexibility. Sticking to strict lessons would be impossible and ineffective. So I strive for an organic flow in my classroom by staying in tune with student needs, while being aware of exactly what needs to be accomplished in the allotted block or week.

As I've mentioned, connecting with students is a primary focus for me. I believe students and teachers can develop a trusting and meaningful relationship. In the ebb and flow of the classroom, my students remind me to "chill" sometimes, and I remind them to straighten up when needed. I love the challenge of keeping up with teenagers on a daily basis, learning about their constantly changing interests and obsessions, comforting them on some days, laying down the line on others, and always listening without judgment.

Flipping my classes has worked well for my personality. I can take my need for structure and offload most of that to homework, allowing the classroom to feel free-flowing. In-class time is based on students' questions—which change from class to class. As teachers, we know that the classroom changes very much from year to year (Actually, I should say block to block!), based on the set of students that you have. Students get to interact with my rigid, structured self *outside* of the classroom and get a much more compassionate, flexible teacher face-to-face.

To me, teaching is all about listening to the students and observing their needs. This is how I feel I gain their trust and respect. So even though I love planning in advance, I know that some of my plans will be thrown out the window or need to be tweaked along the way. In fact, when first making my flipped classroom videos, I refused to make too large a batch over the summer. Why? Because there is so much to learn from the students and so

> A quote from a student when asked to provide two key pieces of advice they would offer to future students:
>
> *I'd say first is trust in your teacher, because Ms. Roshan is really great—which, if you're a new student, I'm sure you'll come to know. She is always available to you, and you need to just trust that she will do her best to get you through it. And second is communicate if you are having an issue. This also has to do with using Ms. Roshan. She is always available, and she's just always in constant communication with you to make sure that you're on top of your game. I'd say those are things that you need to be successful in this class.*

much insight they can provide. In making my Algebra 2 videos, I laid out the structure for my year over the summer and outlined all PowerPoint lessons for the year. This was my scope and sequence planning. I then recorded about three weeks of content over the summer. In that first month of school, I observed how students were watching the videos, what needed to be changed, what things I should keep, and adjusted the next batch of videos accordingly. About three months in, I did a survey of student satisfaction and further adjusted. And now, even though I'm reusing videos that I created in the past, I re-edit the videos from year to year. Nothing should remain static in teaching.

My advice: Identify what you love about teaching and what you'd like to see more of in your class. From there, consider what technology could help you accomplish your goals. Remember that technology is only powerful when you use it well. It is my hope that more and more teachers will look to the tech with whole-child well-being in mind. It is through that lens that we can discover ways to humanize the classroom through the intentional integration of technology into the design of our lessons. In doing so, we can gather powerful information about individual students' needs. And if you decide to try flipping your class, get your camera ready.

It is my hope that more and more teachers will look to the tech with whole-child well-being in mind. It is through that lens that we can discover ways to humanize the classroom through the intentional integration of technology into the design of our lessons.

INTERACTIVITY & MONITORING

Learning checks embedded quizzes

Callout boxes highlights pointers

Quizzes are not meant for grading

Self-assessment with immediate feedback

05

It All Started with a Video

Do the best you can until you know better.
Then when you know better, do better.

—Maya Angelou

*D*iscovering Camtasia back in 2010 changed everything for my class. Instantly, my classroom time could revolve around the students—their questions and their needs for the day. Standing at the board lecturing *at* the students for thirty minutes is not ideal, in my opinion. When students watch the lecture portion of the lesson at home, the classroom becomes a much more dynamic place for all of us. I'm then able to use the data I receive as students engage with the video and respond to questions to decide what to focus on in the classroom.

Keeping Students Focused during Video Lessons

When creating video lessons, it is important to be mindful of the question: How do you capture and keep students' attention during the screencast? Here are some strategies that have worked well for me:

1. Give students something to do.

I have students take notes while watching videos. To me, simply asking them to view a video is not enough; they need to be doing something to fully process. I have students take notes on an outline that I hand out in class. (Tip: make sure any note sheets you hand out have plenty of blank white space for students to write neatly.) As I ink on the screencast, students take their own notes. This handout then serves as a reference in class the next day.

2. Ask questions in your videos.

Just because students can't talk to you during the lesson doesn't mean that you shouldn't be asking questions. It's important to weave in questions that will serve as a basis for class discussion the next day, to prompt students to start thinking analytically about the material. I've found that simply posing a question in a video lecture gets students thinking, questioning, and wondering. You might also consider asking students to jot down their thoughts, whether it be on paper, on a discussion board, in a Google Form, or using some other software or platform, such as Edpuzzle, that allows for it. (In Chapter 6, when I talk about using Edpuzzle to gather homework analytics, you'll see powerful feedback from my students indicating the importance of embedded quizzes.)

3. Pause the video.

Personally, I use Edpuzzle to add interactive elements into my videos. I can embed "comments" to force the video to pause and quiz questions that require students to respond before the video will resume. These pauses help students stay engaged and re-focus them immediately if their mind begins to wander.

4. Don't just talk!

Point, write, highlight, etc. It's important to be doing something to keep students focused in on what's happening. Doing a voiceover on top of a PowerPoint with loads of text is probably not going to keep students' attention. Make your lesson both visual and auditory. If you're reading a long word problem, use a highlighted cursor to skim over the text that you're reading and underline/circle key information as you read.

5. Keep it natural.

Don't worry about making things too professional looking or sounding. You don't want to sound like you're reading from a script, and too many things popping up all over the place just ends up being distracting!

Using Other Teachers' Resources

It would be unreasonable to think that teaching a class requires creating everything from scratch. As teachers, we have certain strengths and passions, and I believe that we should channel time and energy into these areas—and fill the areas where we aren't as strong with others' tools and resources. I genuinely enjoy creating the videos, and because I spend my time there, I frequently look to other teachers' in-class assignments/projects for ideas. I also know there are many teachers who aren't excited about creating

Tips: Creating Effective Flipped Classroom Videos

1. Lay out the structure.

You want to go into your screencast with a plan of action. Remember, these lessons should be concise and to the point. You do not need to write a script (in fact, I never do—I find this is unnatural for me), but you do want to lay out the structure of your lessons.

2. Be neat.

Be clear in your workflow so that students can follow. Be conscious of how you are using your screen space, just as you are when writing on the board in the classroom. You want students to be able to look back at what you've written and for them to be able to follow the work.

3. Use colors.

It's helpful to change colors when inking a screencast. Since you won't be pointing to things as you would in a lesson, you want a way to draw attention and highlight changes. Using colors can be a very helpful way to do this and can keep things neat and clean for students to follow and look back over.

4. Use cursor highlight.

Again, you cannot point during a screencast, but you do want a way for students' eyes to be focusing in on what you're looking at or writing. Here is where using a program that offers a cursor highlight or laser pointer option can be very helpful. I use this feature throughout most of my screencasts. If I'm reading through a problem, I drag my cursor over the text that I'm reading, highlighting key information as I go. And when solving equations, I similarly keep this feature turned on. I've found that it helps students focus on the right part of the screen.

5. Give students something to do while watching the video.

As I mentioned in my tips to keep students focused, I have students take notes while watching videos. I hand out a PowerPoint lesson (hard copy) to students ahead of time that follows the structure I use for my screencast. The handout includes key definitions and has the problems written out. There is also lots of blank white space. As students watch me write in the video, they take notes on their own handout. These notes are what students have on their desk in class while they are working problems the next day.

videos for their courses. For those teachers, making videos could be a barrier that keeps them from adopting the flipped model, but it doesn't have to be. I know many teachers have successfully used videos I have created to get started in implementing the flipped classroom model. One of the most rewarding stories came from a teacher who was assigned to teach AP Calculus at the last minute. She wrote me early in the school year about using my videos in her classroom.

> The amount of prep work for the other classes and cal-culus quickly overwhelmed me, so I started searching for some other solutions. This is when I found your vid-eos, and they have been a godsend. They have enabled me to spend my time doing the homework, figuring out how much to assign, and freed time to research what I needed to do from an AP perspective. I have been able to make it work even though we are follow-ing [a different textbook] ... I look forward to creating my own videos and incorporating this method into my other classes. Again, thank you so much!!

By using my existing videos, the teacher who wrote me that note was able to focus her energy where she needed to—in the classroom. What we do in the classroom is the most important part of the work that we do. The beauty of the internet is that it allows us to draw on other teachers' work—to inspire, to guide, and to use as a ready tool.

Perhaps even more impactful was a note from a student who also had a teacher who had discovered my YouTube channel and had been assigning my videos for homework. I think the note speaks for itself:

Hello, my name is _____. I've commented on a few of your videos, and I have to say, they are really easy to follow and understand. I am a Junior in _____'s AP Calculus class, and most nights we are given the assignment to watch a particular video, write specific notes (plus more if we want more info), and sometimes take an online quiz.

[T]his is [my teacher's] first year teaching this way, with discussions being held about the contents of your videos. We have recently completed chapter two of your videos and having taken a test on it today. I feel that your videos covered everything that was needed in the most efficient way possible! I know I got a good grade on it. :)

Anyways, I'm really enjoying the type of class that I'm in, and it's great that we have access to all of your videos! By the way, our textbook is the same one your videos are based around, which has been really critical if we wish to have more practice.

Thank you so much!

There have been many conversations about the effectiveness of using "other people's" videos in the flipped classroom. My belief is that as long as the teacher is thoughtful about what videos are assigned and how class time is structured around the content of that video, looking to pre-made videos is a great idea. I believe it is essential that the teacher puts his or her own "beginning" and "ending" flow to the video (i.e., class discussion → video with proper assignment → class discussion and follow-up work → next video). But again, I believe that we need to be intentional about where we focus our energy.

The Homework Debate

I have seen so many conversations about homework recently. As I've just talked about using videos that a teacher has curated, rather than created, I thought I might just briefly put this idea out there. In general, we are assigning more and more homework to kids, and that's a huge problem. But I wonder what conversations we need to be having about the *type* of homework being assigned.

When I was sending students home with ten problems to do for homework, there were so many variables in determining how long a student would take to complete that work. Students who require a collaborative working environment to process new ideas might always need to call a friend to complete their math homework. Or students who have slower math processing would consistently take more time than their peers to complete the work. One thing that I've noticed in assigning video lessons is that there is much less variability in the time it takes students to complete this work start to finish, including answering the embedded questions within the video.

In this great debate on homework, it would be beneficial to shift the focus from how many problems to assign to what the homework looks like and how class time is spent (and feedback/help on homework provided). Let's go back to the reason for the homework and the purpose of our class time.

One of the most important things I have learned in the tech work I do with teachers is that when a colleague comes to me asking for a very specific tool, instead of just showing them several websites that can do what they are asking, I need to start by asking them to walk me through the assignment. In many instances, they are taking a project they have been doing for years and looking to upgrade it by infusing technology. Incorporating technology is great, but with that goal as the focus, teachers can miss out on greater opportunities. When I take a step back and ask teachers about the project and goals they are trying to achieve, we often end up in quite a different place than if I had just suggested a tool immediately. It's this rethink of the project with the knowledge of the technology available that takes the project to the next level.

So as we have conversations about time restrictions on homework, how can we talk about shifts to class time and what homework means? This shift will not be immediate and will be a process of change. But I think it is necessary for us to consider the changing needs of our students in order to identify the tools we can embrace to help them learn in whole new ways. The way they interact with the world, communicate, and form relationships is changing. We need to recognize this and be a part of the change too.

The Power of a Teacher's Compassion

I vividly remember my tenth-grade AP Calculus BC teacher, Ms. Escatell. She listened to and observed students and had a gentle touch, even though her course was such a challenging one. In all honesty, I often felt intimidated in the class just because it moved at such a fast pace. (Looking back, I think my parents would have advised me against choosing the super accelerated path I was placed into. Although I was capable of handling the course, there was no need for the ultra-acceleration. I was working my butt off; staying up until one in the morning or later was a normal thing. Perhaps it shouldn't have been.)

Back to my BC Calculus class. I often felt intimidated in the class. Even though I handled the material quite well, I had a hard time keeping up in the classroom. Everything was presented on the overhead projector so quickly, and my classmates seemed to all be absorbing the information instantaneously. But I wasn't. In class, I had mindlessly jotted down everything the teacher was writing on the board, but I couldn't process at the speed the teacher spoke. So each evening, before I could actually begin the assigned textbook homework, I had to first process and make sense of all my notes. (Remembering that time I spent on schoolwork each evening is a huge reason why I developed my flipped classroom when I started teaching AP Calculus.) I wasn't incapable of understanding the material, but I needed time to synthesize and absorb the information. Looking back, I can't believe that no one realized this. I think it was just because I always did so well in school. If I was getting grades at the top of the class, then clearly there wasn't a problem. Right?

Wrong!

I do have to thank Ms. Escatell for being such a kind and caring teacher. One particular memory of her has stuck with me through the years. I had gotten myself so worked up and nervous about the midterm exam that I had also studied all night and only gotten two hours of sleep. The day of the exam, I worked so slowly through it all that time was up before I knew what had happened—leaving a large section completely untouched. Later, before my teacher returned the exams, she sat with me and told me that she knew something must have been up on the day of the exam because my performance was so atypical. She told me that I could complete the portion of the exam that I had not gotten to. That meant the world to me. It's something I will never forget.

As a teacher, I still remember that compassion, and I afford similar opportunities to my students. You never know what is going on with a kid. Kindness and empathy are critical in teaching. If you know your students well enough, you know when to extend these opportunities.

EMPOWER ALL STUDENTS

introvert OR extrovert

fast OR slow

ACTIVE PARTICIPANTS
IN THEIR LEARNING

06

Using Edtech to Empower Every Student to Speak Up

A tool is only a tool until it is part of a solution.

When students come to my class for the first time, they immediately notice two things: first, it's flipped, and second, it's a rigorous, fast-paced course. Both of these facts make my class seem a little different—which can initially be scary for some—so it's imperative for me to quickly gain students' trust and give them the confidence that the classroom is going to be built around them and customized to their needs. Students need to know that I am there to listen, not only to their math questions but also to their concerns, frustrations, and worries.

I do that, at least in part, by using technology to connect and communicate with students. When considering whether to use a particular tool, I ask myself a few questions:

- How is this going to help me get to know my students better?
- Is this going to help me individualize instruction?
- Is it going to help me customize feedback?

If my answer is yes to any of the questions above, I've probably experimented with the tool. The edtech tools I'm most interested in are those that help me analyze processes, get quick results, and give instant feedback to students. In this section, I will share some of the tools I've chosen—and why—and explain how I use the information I collect to inform the way I structure lessons, create groups, and target individual and class needs.

My goal in this chapter is not to simply expose you to a bunch of the tech tools I use. My hope is that, rather than focusing on the tool, I can give you a snapshot of its impact on my classroom and teaching. It isn't the tools themselves that brought my classroom to where it is today. Rather, it was the challenges I faced and the questions I asked that helped me find the right technology solutions for the problems I wanted to solve.

I've already noted some of the essential questions I ask myself when reflecting on potential changes in my classroom or technology I'm considering. But the questions can change. Intentional

> It isn't the tools themselves that brought my classroom to where it is today. Rather, it was the challenges I faced and the questions I asked that helped me find the right technology solutions for the problems I wanted to solve.

reflection helps me find the answers and the right technology for my students. By asking simple questions, including what is going well, what areas could use improvement, what I wish I had more time for, and where connections with my students are lacking, I can find areas for growth. When I have identified the personal and academic goals I am trying to achieve, I'm able to examine available tech tools and consider which might be key in helping me achieve those goals. Lists of tools are great to have on hand, but I really try to start with the reflective process. I hope that what follows will help you engage in a similar practice.

Using Technology to Personalize Learning

When I first began flipping my math classroom in 2010, the ability to screencast, upload to the web, and give students the option to watch lectures at their own pace was exciting and innovative. Creating video lessons helped me move toward a more personalized, student-centered classroom, but it was only the first step in that direction. New tech tools that have emerged in the past five years have revolutionized what is possible. I want to focus on three that transformed my teaching: Pear Deck, Zaption,[1] and

> While the tools themselves did not change my classroom, the potential to get such detailed information on how students process material, as well as the immediacy of feedback, has transformed how I teach.

1 Unfortunately, Zaption was acquired a couple years back and is no longer available. There are alternative tools (I have since transitioned to Edpuzzle, which is an overall great option), but it was the Zaption team's vision that was truly transformative to my teaching.

Flipgrid. While the tools themselves did not change my classroom, the potential to get such detailed information on how students process material, as well as the immediacy of feedback, has transformed how I teach. The insight these tools gave me allowed me to differentiate instruction, empower students with a better understanding of their own comprehension, emphasize process and reflection, and gain a new awareness of classroom needs.

Using Zaption/Edpuzzle to Gather Homework Analytics

My students typically watch a video for homework so we can engage in discussion and critical thinking tasks in the classroom. Over the years, I have grown to rely on both interactivity and monitoring in the videos I assign for homework. Empowered with this information, I can customize and personalize the learning experience for each student in the classroom.

As I mentioned above, Zaption was the tool that transformed my flipped classroom. Now that their tool is no longer available, I use Edpuzzle, which I will refer to for the most part from this point forward.

Edpuzzle is a site that allows teachers to select a video and customize it by editing, cropping, recording audio, and adding questions to make an engaging and interactive lesson. I assign each of my videos through Edpuzzle and embed questions within the video. Students can watch the video at home, and teachers can access details, such as when the student watched, areas a student skipped or had to rewind, and answers to the free-response and multiple-choice questions the teacher has embedded.

For each of the flipped classroom videos I make, I load it up in Edpuzzle and embed quizzes and text boxes. Edpuzzle helps transform a passive video watching experience into a more active one. I use the various question types Edpuzzle provides for different purposes. For example, the multiple-choice questions I ask yield immediate, automated feedback, for both the student and for me. This helps students self-assess as they watch the video and provides me a quick snapshot of areas that need more attention and follow-up in the classroom. The short-answer-type questions I ask, on the other hand, give students the opportunity to dig a bit deeper and to assess beyond recognition. I find this question type helpful when asking more inquiry-based questions, which can provide a nice segue into class discussion the following day. This is also the area where students can leave me more detailed questions they have or write a note about something they want me to address in the classroom. I use this data to set the tone for full-class discussion, to group students based on need, and to pre-identifying necessary one-on-one work.

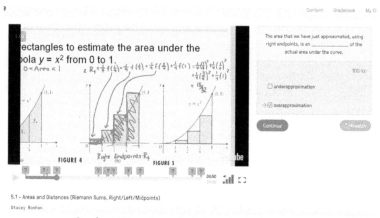

Student View: Sample Edpuzzle Assignment

It is also possible to simply add in a text box that pauses the video (but does not require the student to answer a question before proceeding). I use text boxes to zone students' attention and provide a visual cue to important talking points. Much like margin notes or highlighted definitions are used in a textbook, text boxes can be used to call attention to key concepts. Since these text boxes force the video to pause, I strategically place them to focus students' attention and help them summarize the notes they are taking on the video.

In addition to the data from the quizzes themselves, Edpuzzle tracks how much of the video a student has watched and even shows what areas a student watched two or three times. This can be helpful data in identifying how long students are spending on the video and how they are processing the material. I have definitely come to rely on this statistic.

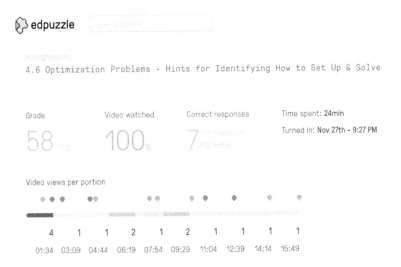

Before students even step into the classroom, Edpuzzle's analytics inform how I should run class the next day and alert me to individual student needs immediately. I can then design learning tasks customized to the needs of the class, create the most effective student pairings, and identify student-leaders to facilitate peer-to-peer learning.

The ability to monitor student progress is extremely powerful for the teacher. But real-time feedback is just as important for the student. Embedded quizzes give students the opportunity to check their understanding immediately. And short-answer questions can be used to guide the students to make big-picture connections, summarize concepts, or take a reflective pause. Not only does the interactivity engage students, it forces them to think more critically and understand areas where they need to focus questions. This way, students can make the most effective use of their class time.

When I first began embedding quizzes into my videos, I did a survey with my students, asking them a series of questions about how they liked the flipped classroom videos and, more specifically, if they found the embedded quizzes and callout boxes helpful.

What do you like most about the video lessons so far?

- "I can ask you questions when I'm doing the problems in class, so now I'm not trapped at home totally confused beyond repair anymore."
- "When I don't understand some problems, I can always go back and watch it again."
- "I can watch at my own pace, pause and take notes, and ask questions in class on material I did not understand."
- "I really like that I come to class everyday with solid notes." (Keep in mind that I ask students to fill out the PowerPoint that I print and hand out in class, which serves as their notes in class the next day.)
- "I like to see you work out each problem step-by-step and explain what you're doing during it." (Note: I ink and talk in real time [not a voiceover of a pre-written solution], and I think this is important.)

Do you find the embedded quizzes helpful?

- "They test my knowledge of what I have learned already in the video, as well as what I should be picking up from the video. I think it is really important that I am quizzed because then I can really know what I should be taking out of the video."
- "I find that it helps me take a quick moment to reflect on what I have just heard/watched in the video. This allows me to gather my thoughts, stay focused, and test my knowledge of the topic."
- "I feel like they keep me listening extra carefully if I see a question about to come up. I also think the questions tend to highlight important things we must know. These can be helpful if you need to go back to a video if you have a question on something. The questions in the video can show you where in the video your own question may be answered."
- "Yes, I can see right away what I understand and what I don't."
- "They make me pay attention."
- "It reinforces what is really important for us to know and take out of the videos."

Do you find the text boxes (the blue boxes that pop up and pause the video) helpful?

- "Yes, because they have important clarifying information. I know I have to pay attention to what is on the screen when it pauses."
- "Yes. They really stress some key tips or reminders that could be helpful in the future. If I'm zoning out, then the pause wakes me up again."
- "Yes, because after watching the video for so long, it helps me a lot when something pops up on the screen."

- "Yes, it makes sure I am still involved and forces me to press play to resume."
- "Yes! I always write them down with a star next to them because I know they're really important."

How Zaption Transformed My Teaching

As my flipped classroom evolved, embedding quizzes into my video lessons became a major component of how I run my class. Zaption was a game changer for me, and it is, hands down, one of my favorite edtech tools ever. Why? Zaption allowed me to form deep, meaningful connections with my students. I am not trying to exaggerate; this is truly what I feel. Let me explain.

Zaption allowed me to get a sense of individual and class needs before students even walked into the classroom. Each evening, I would log into the Zaption analytics for the homework video I had assigned. Zaption was so simple and so clear, yet gave the perfect detail to target what I needed to zone in on. I never walked into the classroom without analyzing student responses. To me, reviewing these answers was an extremely important part of my class prep. It equipped me with such valuable information that, in turn, made my time in the classroom more meaningful.

A truly standout feature of Zaption was the "responses" display and the ability to show/hide student names. At the beginning of each class, I would project questions, along with the anonymous answers, from the class on the board.

The display included the "video content," specifying the spot in the video where the question was asked (which really cued students' memory back to the video), the choices, a chart or word cloud to get an overall sense of how the class responded, and individual answers. By starting class going over the video in this way, students were better able to connect the lesson of the day to the video homework. The questions I ask in the video are the basis for class discussion. Before I started using Zaption, some students struggled to make the connection between homework and classwork. Zaption broke down this disconnect. This was huge.

On an individual level, I feel like Zaption helped me build trust and stronger relationships with my students. I made it a point to always include some open-ended questions in Zaption and always read everything that each student had written. In class, I would talk to individual students whose responses called for that—i.e., if a student's answer clearly indicated confusion, if a student asked a question unrelated to what I had asked (but something they needed me to talk to them about), or if a student left a witty reply, I'd follow up on that. Students *knew* that I was reading what they wrote. In evaluation forms, students would comment that I always took the time to thoroughly review all of their homework and, to them, that translated to how much I cared.

Zaption made me efficient and effective in targeting what my students needed most from me and allowed me to get to know my students in ways I simply could not have accomplished without the technology. Though I haven't seen another tool for video inter-activity that hits it out of the park like Zaption, there are certainly other tools that achieve the same main goals. As I mentioned pre-viously, I now use Edpuzzle.

Using Pear Deck to Kick Off Class Discussion

One of my favorite ways to kick off classroom discussion is using Pear Deck, a formative assessment tool that allows teachers to ask questions within a presentation and display the responses of the class on the board anonymously. I create a guided activity to ramp students up to thinking about and answering bigger-picture ques-tions. Pear Deck requires each student to engage and respond and allows me to gauge the tone of the classroom, see where students are making connections, and immediately identify who needs what for the day. In a traditional class discussion, students must raise their hands to respond and might be conscious of what their peers think of their answer. Pear Deck removes this barrier by displaying student work without names attached (teachers can go back later to a separate dashboard to review by individual). Thus, the class can talk about and analyze the incorrect answers without calling any individual student out.

To further differentiate, I use Pear Deck's Student-Paced Mode. Traditional classroom discussions often pressure students into quickly responding, or may lead to quick assumptions that a student who is responding slowly does not know the material as well as a peer who immediately raises her hand. With Pear Deck's Student-Paced Mode, students can work through problems at their own pace. I can monitor progress through the dashboard, in real time, so I can target individual needs at the same time I am looking at the overall class analytics. This information allows me to move throughout the classroom efficiently and effectively and sit down with individuals to provide the precise help they need.

Students should have the opportunity to respond in a format that is most comfortable for them. While some are naturally more vocal, others thrive when they have a moment to process and type out their thoughts. Pear Deck gives the quiet and quick students and the louder and more methodical students equal voice. After each student has responded, I can project all answers on the board for a group discussion. This dialogue is an important part of my class, and using tools such as Pear Deck allows me to ask the question differently and to get a far better sense of individual needs than I ever could before.

> **Students should have the opportunity to respond in a format that is most comfortable for them.**

On the classroom management end, it's important to create slides where students are continuously engaged and interacting with the content on their screen. The way I set up my Pear Deck requires students to actively participate on each slide, so they don't have time to get too distracted by other things on their laptop. Another area I focus on early in the year is getting into an efficient routine. When students walk into the room and see a Pear Deck join code on the board, they know they need to get their computer out and get logged in immediately. Class time is valuable, and we don't have time to waste waiting for everyone to log in. In my experience, by creating a healthy routine and clear expectations early on, you will save yourself many minutes in the long run.

My flipped classroom has evolved and continues to transform as tech tools provide new and exciting ways to get insight into individual and class needs. Pear Deck allows me to provide a level of personalization and customization that simply was not possible just five years ago.

How Pear Deck Transformed My Teaching

In my classroom, I mainly use Pear Deck as a warm-up activity. (In the next section of this book, when I talk about my online class, you will see how critical Pear Deck has been in how I run synchronous sessions.) The Pear Deck activity gets students going and energized, but it also gives me a quick snapshot of where everyone in the classroom is in terms of understanding. I can collect very detailed information on student progress instantaneously, without having to call on them, and I'm not swayed by the most vocal student setting the tone for where all students are with the material. Pear Deck also gives the quiet students in the classroom, the ones that you don't particularly want to call out in the middle of class, an opportunity to answer and throw valuable contribution into the discussion. This is precisely the tool I would have dreamed of having when I was in school, so I could get my thoughts out "on paper" before having to verbalize that idea, so I could have had time to process what I was thinking, so that I didn't need to raise my hand and hold all my thoughts in my head until I was finally called on. On the teacher end, when using Pear Deck, I can anonymously display all student work on the classroom projector. This allows us to discuss why there might be confusion around a topic or to highlight common errors. Having actual student responses displayed, anonymously, adds great value to our discussion about the question. In the next section, Addressing Diverse Student Needs Using Pear Deck, I talk in detail about how Pear Deck allows us to talk about mistakes without calling any individual student out and has helped me reduce the need for hand-raising in the classroom.

Using Flipgrid to Allow Students to Verbalize Their Thought Process and Reflect

If you can't explain it simply, you don't understand it well enough.
—Albert Einstein

One of my biggest goals in teaching is simply to provide enough opportunity to hear students talk. There is tremendous power in listening in on what students are saying, hearing how they are thinking through the process of solving problems, and giving them the space to just chat things out with their peers. I believe that students learn so much in the act of talking things through. So do we as adults!

For a while now, I have had students create video solutions to math questions in my AP Calculus class, and they tended to be rather formal in nature. The goal was that students would create a screencast solving a problem they had been assigned, and then I would post all of these video solutions for the class to learn from. Before students recorded, they would get their answer checked by me so I could make sure that there weren't errors being presented in the videos. I knew this was a very valuable assignment—there is huge merit in students teaching one another—but this type of activity takes a while and is hard to build in as a weekly one.

This is where I turned to Flipgrid to revamp what I had done in the past. Instead of having students make a fancy screencast, I decided to have students just talk about math solutions by hovering their phone's camera over their piece of paper. With the Flipgrid app, students can use both the front-facing and rear-facing camera on their phone when creating a recording. What I asked my students to do was this:

Instructions

Pick a question that you found challenging in this chapter but that you feel you now understand. On a piece of paper, carefully and precisely write out:

- the question
- your solution to the problem

On your phone, open the Flipgrid App.

- In the Flipgrid App, enter code: xxx, which will take you to the "xxx" topic.
- Hit "+ Add your response" at the bottom of the screen to add your video response.
- You will have three minutes to record your response. Please alternate between using your front camera to record your lovely face and the back camera to record your handwritten work, as in my example.
- Press the record button to begin recording.
  - Start with the camera on your face as you introduce the problem.
  - When you are ready to start talking about your solution, switch your camera view to the rear-facing camera and hover your phone over your handwritten work.
  - You can press the pause button at any point, as needed.

- Press next when you are done recording and review your response.
- For your thumbnail, use a picture of just your face or a snapshot of your solution.

You can find a direct link to this Flipgrid activity, which you can copy and modify for your own needs, on the resources page of my website at techiemusings.com/techwithheart.

With this activity, I am able to hear how students are analyzing problems. When students hand in a worksheet, I can see the series of steps they followed, but I am not able to hear their approach or the justification for the process they chose. By asking students to instead *record* a solution, I can better target individual needs by seeing which steps have been glossed over and how students are making connections to big-picture ideas.

The goal of this activity depends on when in the learning cycle it is assigned. If the task is assigned while students are first learning the material (i.e., instead of assigning ten problems as homework, I will ask them to focus on just one problem and create a Flipgrid explanation to that question), then I typically just respond with feedback to each student on their work. If a student creates an exemplary explanation, I will share that with the class; but typically, at this point, students are still learning and developing their understandings. The goal of this assignment is for me to hear the students' process in solving the problem and for me to gain a better understanding of any misconceptions.

If this task is assigned after we have spent a couple days on a topic, or as review leading up to an assessment, the goal shifts a bit. At this point, I expect students to have built a deeper understanding of the concepts, and they have the resources needed to create thoughtful video explanations that can be used to teach others. When a Flipgrid is assigned at this point, I have the class review the videos their classmates have made. Students then respond to one or two videos they watched and focus on topics they could use reinforcement in. I give them some prompts to help guide their reply, such as the following:

- What did this video help clarify?
- What was really strong about the video solution you watched?
- Do you have any suggestions for ways this video could be improved? Would you have done anything differently in solving this problem?
- What are your major takeaways from the problem you saw solved or the approach your classmate took to solving this problem?

The type of task mentioned above is also one that we use often in our final month of "AP prep." Having students create and critique in this way is a powerful activity as we synthesize material spanning the scope of the course.

The magic in using Flipgrid is how easy it is to do assignments like these. Students simply use the technology they all have in their pockets—a smartphone. There are no fancy tablets or downloads necessary. Open the app and press record! And for me, I don't need to upload any recordings or share individual projects on a class page. Within the grid I set up, students can view all of their classmates' videos.

Flipgrid has helped me accomplish my goals of building collaboration and community, helping students verbalize their math, and seeing and hearing from all students. It's actually pretty amazing to see how some of the quieter students find their voice in these Flipgrid activities. I think some of it comes down to processing speed, being able to script and practice a response before posting (it's fun to observe which students speak off the cuff versus those who have clearly rehearsed), level of shyness, etc. I will say that, for some students, the first couple of Flipgrid assignments are nerve-wracking and intimidating. But by making this a constant in the course and repeating the activity on a regular basis, I have found that students quickly get into a routine and become comfortable with the activity. I think it's helpful that the first several we do are private between me and the student[2] so that they can build this level of confidence. Again, I repeat to them that nothing about this exercise is meant to be "perfect" or "polished." The goal is to hear my students think through problems, force them to verbalize their reasoning, and to hear a bit of each student's personality in the process. This assignment is such an easy way to achieve these goals.

How Flipgrid Transformed My Teaching

Flipgrid opened up a way for me to really emphasize to my students the idea of "process over product." I am always looking for ways to better see how students are reasoning through problems. How many times do we figure out a solution to a problem by simply going to a peer and asking for their help, only to discover that in the process of lively discussion, we arrive at the solution ourselves? There is a lot of power in simply talking things out.

As I mentioned earlier, I immediately discovered how easily I could assign and collect video responses from my students without asking them to purchase any fancy equipment, download software, or even create an account. In playing around with the Flipgrid app on my iPhone, I thought to myself, "What better way to have students informally reason their way through a math solution than by using a device they all have in their pockets?"

---

2 An easy way to keep videos private in Flipgrid is to simply turn on "Video Moderation" when setting up your Flipgrid topic. After students submit their recording, you can choose whether to activate submissions for the full class to see or not from your teacher admin dashboard. All videos remain private and viewable to the teacher only until they are activated.

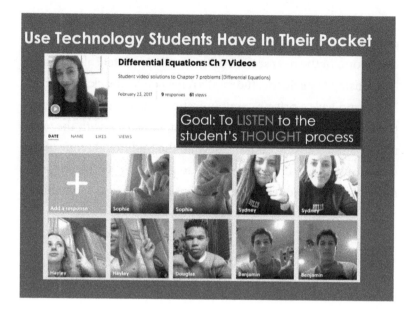

In having students do more of these Flipgrid activities toward the end of the unit, as they began to review and connect the dots between individual sections in the chapter, I found that I was giving students the opportunity to both be a teacher and also deepen their understanding of concepts from the perspective of their peers. I truly believe that there is no better way to learn than by teaching. One of the most powerful aspects of having technology in the classroom is the ability to connect and give our students a louder voice and a larger community of learners to talk to. By creating assignments where I asked students to become the

> I truly believe that there is no better way to learn than by teaching.

teacher, students were required to both think critically about their solution process and become empathetic toward how students viewing their content might receive their explanation.

As I discovered the power of seeing my students speak on camera, I started making Flipgrid activities a normal part of my classroom. In the next section of this book, I will talk about how I began using Flipgrid for students to reflect on feedback, learn from "fails," and have a private communication channel to ask me questions outside of the classroom. Yet again, in playing with the technology and creatively thinking beyond the traditional scope of the tool, I was able to find another way to give students the opportunity to open up and tell me more about themselves as individuals.

07

Pedagogy > Tech

Much of the world, from school to the workplace, is set up to reward extroverts, and therefore it can be easier for introverts to feel overlooked or as if they don't measure up. For instance, even if you know all the answers but don't want to call attention to yourself by raising your hand, you might end up feeling, or being perceived as, less smart than the kids flailing their arms to get the teacher's attention. Same goes for work. Just remember, as Susan Cain writes in Quiet, "There's zero correlation between being the best talker and having the best ideas."

—Sophia Amoruso, #GIRLBOSS

*P*encils down, time's up.
  Capture all multiples of five before the timer is up.
  Game over!

In elementary school, I felt as if I was always being timed in math. And I could never finish in time. Tests made me panic, I had to count on my fingers and toes, and my friend was always faster than me when we practiced flashcards. My teachers told me that I didn't know the material well enough and my friend was smarter. And I believed them.[1]

To top this all off, I was a perfectionist. I wanted to raise my hand and participate, but uncertainty, combined with the time-sensitive pressure to be the first to raise my hand and be called on, was oftentimes too much. And so, even though I was always eager to participate, it may not have always seemed this way to my teachers.

I decided early on in my teaching that I wanted to reduce the stress level in my classroom. It's why I flipped my classroom, after all. As I've looked to technology to help me reimagine how class runs, I have been very deliberate in my approach. I'm careful to dissect the problem and need before jumping to the tech. Thinking back to my own experiences in school and how I felt in the classroom has led me to focus on these driving questions:

- How can we create safe learning environments for all students to find their voice and build their confidence?
- How can we leverage technology to gain insight into student needs and provide them multiple ways of showcasing their understanding and expressing themselves?
- How can we empower students with the resources they need to take ownership for their learning?

1 Jo Boaler talks extensively about the need to stop this timed-testing madness. (See the article "Research Suggests Timed Tests Cause Math Anxiety" for more information.) I'm so grateful to her for bringing this conversation to the forefront. Timed tests and math anxiety are two topics that clearly hit so close to home for me.

Let me take you through the process of choosing some of the key tools in my flipped classroom…

Because I flipped my class, students are able to watch a video for homework at a pace that best fits them. Students can pause and rewind the video based on how they are grasping the lesson. They can look back at old videos as they work to synthesize the material and make connections. In class, instead of standing at the board to deliver what *I* need to cover for the day, I can sit with individuals and customize class to their needs. Though this was a start, I realized that I could embrace tech tools to make the video watching experience a more active exercise for my students. And this is where I turned to Edpuzzle. Students now have the chance to self-assess as they watch, and I come to class equipped with the analytics from the video so I can pre-identify what needs to be done for the day. In class, students work on problems in groups, collaboratively, at a pace that suits them. They have plenty of time in the classroom to get problems solved and questions answered and to chat about their process, reasoning, and thoughts. When I want to engage the class in a full discussion, I usually do this through Pear Deck so that no student can be a passive participant. Students have time to process and respond to the question on their own computer screen. They can contribute without needing to raise their hand, and we can discuss mistakes without singling any child out.

I'm always on a mission to find tools that help me get to know my students as individuals and build meaningful relationships with them. The information that both Edpuzzle and Pear Deck provide through the teacher dashboard gives me the ability to amplify student learning and give each student a voice in the classroom. These tools allow me to hear from each and every student in the room.

Technology provides a powerful way to engage students, inform individual and group instruction, differentiate lessons, document work, and empower students to direct their own learning. But if you want technology to be a transformative force in your classroom, school, or district, you have to start with "why?"

HOW CAN WE...

create

SAFE

learning environments for all students

VOICE

CONFIDENCE

Check out the video at bit.ly/empathyinedtech

If you are interested in seeing how we have approached this question at my school, take a moment to watch this video I created to explain our philosophy at Bullis: "Empathy in EdTech: How We Are Transforming Learning at Bullis" (this video can also be found on the resources page of my website).

As both a teacher and technology integrationist, I know the importance of finding simple solutions that keep the focus on the learning. One way to ensure we start the conversation with the pedagogy is to identify a set of go-to tools we help our students feel comfortable with, then to set a routine where using these tools becomes natural. Maintaining a small suite of tools also helps our students become fluent with technology that will boost their learning and productivity and serve them well in the long run.

Here are the primary reasons Pear Deck, Flipgrid, and Edpuzzle are go-to tools in my classroom:

- They provide each student in the classroom an equal voice. In a traditional classroom discussion, students are called on or raise their hands to respond. As a result, teachers often repeatedly hear from the same students. In contrast, Pear Deck, Flipgrid, and Edpuzzle provide each student an opportunity to respond individually.

- They engage each student in the room. With these tools, each student is required to actively participate and respond to each question, form an opinion, and submit an answer.

- They create a safe space for each student to honestly respond and make mistakes. Students have time to draft out and revise responses before posting them. And the teacher can make answers anonymous to the group so students don't have to worry about how their peers might perceive their answers or worry about answering incorrectly (in Flipgrid, the teacher can choose to turn on moderated posts to keep all videos private to just the teacher).

- They allow educators to efficiently and effectively target class and individual student needs. The analytics provided show class trends and also provide indicators of who is struggling.

- They differentiate how students can respond to questions. While some students are wonderful with oral discussion and on-the-spot responses, other students are best when they have time to process and collect their thoughts before recording or typing an answer.

The Importance of Failing

Failure is part of the learning process. One of the most important parts. But based on my own experiences as a learner, I know there is a fine line between pushing a student in a healthy way and setting up an environment that can be harmful to the student. Clearly, I'm oversensitive on this issue based on my own personal experiences. But this is an important part of the teacher I have become.

Risk-taking and support are two of the most common themes I think of in my teaching. I believe that being a good teacher requires allowing students to safely take risks. That sounds almost oxymoronic. Providing a warm, welcoming classroom environment where students know that their teacher is there to support them is hugely important to me. But equally important is that my students become independent learners, unafraid to jot down equations or play with the numbers even when they are not quite sure where they are headed. Yes, the role of supportive teacher is much more comfortable for me than encouraging real risk-taking. But I also am aware of the fact that there is no way to achieve excellence without failing along the way.

When you remove the fear of failure, impossible things suddenly become possible.
—Regina Dugan

By flipping my class, I was able to give students more control. It was more about my own fears that they would feel anxious or turned off by failure. But flipping my classroom dynamic allowed me to set up a class environment where we took risks together, and I was there to "support" students as they experimented.

I've experienced students who were literally paralyzed with fear of failure (where less than 85 percent equals failure in their mind). I truly believe that earning students' trust and being a constant support allows them to push beyond their comfort zone . . . even if it is more gradual for some than others. The flipped classroom has certainly allowed me to be an observant teacher who gets to know her students as individuals. My students pick up on that vibe, and that's where the relationship-building process begins.

I once saw somebody write: "One can't succeed at any research project of significance without failing along the way (unless you're really lucky)." I'd argue that those who did *not* fail were the unlucky ones. We often learn more in the process of failing than we do when it comes out the right way on the first try. Because what is learning but iterative failure, right?!

Even with the awareness of the importance of failing along the way, fear of anything less than stellar on a transcript can feel devastating to a teen. It can easily influence their willingness to take a course or feel confident about a subject. And again, back to my personal story, I am all too aware of this.

As I've mentioned, I went to a very challenging Math, Science, Computer Science Magnet Middle and High school. Even there, I was placed in the highest, most accelerated math track. My father was strict, and his expectations were (too) high. I'll never forget the A that I proudly brought home on an elementary school quiz that my father looked at with disappointment before asking me what I could have done differently to earn a perfect score. My parents were (and still are) the best parents in the world—as supportive as could be and wanting only the very, very best for their children. Pleasing my father was one of the most important things to me when I was younger. And so, achieving perfect grades was a huge priority in my mind. Too bad I picked just about the most difficult environment in which to achieve this much too high (and unhealthy) standard.

These experiences have shaped my teaching in a variety of ways. Let me start with a brief glimpse into how I felt. I had the most fabulous math education, and I loved math. It was an exciting, exhilarating puzzle. Nothing, and I mean nothing, could ever make me feel differently about math! BUT math classes often caused me to feel anxious and overwhelmed. Nearly all of my teachers pushed me to think outside of the box to a point that was unhealthy given my perfectionist attitude. Only a few teachers made me feel like stumbling along was necessary and expected. To those teachers who took the time to sit me down and explain this to me, I remember you and I thank you. But that was not the message I was hearing so often.

On top of everything, my high school environment was intensely competitive. Some quizzes and tests were meant to be "failed" and curved, but that was a terrifying feeling for me. Nobody was there to let me know that everything didn't need to be perfect. I only remember one teacher who was aware of how nervous I would often get on assessments. I know that I did not often display on the outside what I was feeling on the inside, but if somebody had really gotten to know me, they would have seen through.

My primary goal when I began teaching was to be a supportive, nurturing force in my students' lives. I was determined to make a year in my math class as pleasant an experience as students had ever had. I wanted them to leave the year without feeling scared of math. My goal was to provide the necessary rigor while maintaining a calm, compassionate classroom environment.

The flipped classroom has allowed me to be this teacher. It's been my way of providing students with routine and structure, confidence in their expectations, and a classroom environment where we all are taking risks together. I'm there to pick up on how students are approaching problems and dealing with challenges. I have time to sit down with all my students and give them the space to talk to me if and when they're up for it. My classroom isn't

Dear Ms. Roshan,

Thank you for being an amazing teacher! I look forward to your class every day. You helped me become more confident in myself. You encouraged me to ask more questions and take more risks. By the end of the year, I was not afraid to share my opinions with the rest of the class. I don't think I have ever learned as much as I did in Honors Algebra 2. I hope I have you as a teacher again!

perfect. Whose is? But the flipped classroom has allowed me to make the connections with students that I was striving for. And to me, there is nothing more important than that.

It's Not A Speed Race

I love math. I have *always* loved math. But from elementary school through high school, I didn't always love math class.

As I previously mentioned, in elementary school, I never felt that I shined in math. I was slow, and we constantly had timed tests or flashcard tests of math facts. It wasn't until I was in fifth grade, when my mom started teaching me Algebra 2 in her community college class (where I rocked it), that I started feeling confident. My experience being successful in such a high-level math class in fifth grade changed everything. It was eye-opening for me. When I found my mom's course easy, I gained a whole new level of confidence and realized for the first time how strongly I could connect very complex math concepts. In my mom's math class, it wasn't about learning facts and showing mastery of those facts on a timed test. For the first time, I was being asked to logic my way to discovering new concepts. I still remember thinking that it all felt like putting a puzzle together.

> *A lot of scientific evidence suggests that the difference between those who succeed and those who don't is not the brains they were born with, but their approach to life, the messages they receive about their potential, and the opportunities they have to learn.*
> —Jo Boaler, *Mathematical Mindsets*

Math was totally my thing, but the way math was taught in elementary school didn't really allow me to see this. I ended up really excelling in math in middle and high school. But even there, even in classes where I was doing great, the time pressure caused me constant anxiety.

Providing a Safe Space for All Learners to Actively Participate

My mindset as a student was that everything needed to be perfect; anything less was unacceptable. Taking the risk to raise my hand in class, when I wanted to contribute my thoughts, was always a challenge for me. But none of my teachers ever seemed to recognize this; or, if they did, they never acknowledged it. The thing is, I really wanted to contribute to class discussions. I just didn't always know how to. And on top of my perfectionism, I was slow. Because I did so well in school, nobody was ever concerned; however, from the time I was in elementary school, it was difficult to complete assessments on time, and it always took me unreasonably long to finish homework in the evening.

When I was in grad school, I had a teacher who carried a stack of name cards around the room. As he lectured, he would randomly pick names from the stack to call on students. That class was a nightmare for me. I understand the importance of engaging every student and making sure each child is actively listening. But what these methods can do, especially for a student like me, is cause this constant feeling of being on edge. I could never pay full attention because I always felt on alert. I was scared to be called on. I didn't want to be put on the spot. And it was not so much about being wrong at this point in my education and life. But when called on, you needed to have the answer right then and there. I was an economics major, so most of the answers were not just factual in nature. They required you to synthesize and apply. Now you have to understand, this thinking was a process I really enjoyed. That's why I studied applied economics! But I am not quick. I always read questions more than once, jot down all of the information I am given, and only then do I begin tackling the problem.

To this day, when I want to contribute to discussion, raising my hand makes my heart beat a bit faster. And I often get so busy formulating my response in my head that I tune out the conversation that's happening around me. For example, I was recently in a faculty meeting. I was eager to contribute to the discussion. I let a few people answer before me, but while that was going on, I was scripting in my head what I wanted to say, which completely distracted me from hearing what my peers were saying. This is something I personally work on; it doesn't happen all the time, but it happens often.

Now imagine that class in grad school where the teacher always held notecards in his hand, randomly calling on the next student in the stack. I was constantly rehearsing answers in my head throughout the class period and rarely felt calm. It wasn't even that I didn't know the answer. It was that 1) I need time to process and think and oftentimes coming up with an instant answer was just not possible, and 2) I am a perfectionist and wanted so badly for that answer to be right and impressive.

As teachers, we see it every day—some students are less likely to raise their hand when they have a question or an answer to provide.[2] Or, if they do raise their hand, they may not raise it high and are probably not vocal, which lessens the probability that I will get over to them as soon as they have a question or that they will be called on first. Additionally, some students process more quickly than others, and students who answer questions more slowly may not always have the time needed to form a response.

Because of my experiences as a student, I just don't believe in the practice of cold-calling on students. As a teacher, I am hypersensitive to how students feel during class discussion. From my perspective as a teacher, there is a group of students who always shoot their hands up first, those who are vocal and bold with their questions and answers. And then there are so many who are quiet. Their voices don't get heard in the same way unless the teacher gives them the proper outlet. So I put a lot of effort into making sure that each student has a safe space to contribute. That being said, I do not entirely avoid calling on students. I know the importance of pushing students beyond their comfort zones.

And when it comes to contributing to discussion, this is an extremely important skill that I have to help my students develop. But I go to great lengths to figure out which students might need my support in this area. And I also give ample opportunity for students to contribute to class discussion that does not involve hand-raising or being called on. That leads me to Pear Deck. I was searching for a way to reduce hand-raising in my classroom while still being able to get a sense of individual needs.

---

2 Susan Cain talks about hand-raising in a lot of her research.

Addressing Diverse Student Needs Using Pear Deck

To continue on the topic of how Pear Deck has transformed my teaching, Pear Deck allows me to get to know my students, deepen the personalization I can provide, hear from each and every student in my classroom, and be the most efficient teacher I can be. My favorite use of Pear Deck is as a warm-up tool because it allows each student to contribute an answer without me having to call out any student individually. Three critical components of this warm-up period, and class time overall, are to do the following:

- Engage each learner in the classroom;
- Gauge how students are thinking about bigger picture questions; and
- Give each student in the classroom an opportunity to "talk."

Society often overlooks us introverts. We idolize the talkers and the spotlight seekers, as if they are the role models everyone should be emulating. I call this the Extrovert Ideal. This is the belief that we're all supposed to be quick-thinking, charismatic risk-takers who prefer action to contemplation. The Extrovert Ideal is what can make you feel as if there's something wrong with you because you're not at your best in a large group. It's an especially powerful force in school, where the loudest, most talkative kids are often the most popular, and where teachers reward the students who are eager to raise their hands in class.

—Susan Cain, *Quiet Power*

Pear Deck helps me address the needs of those students who are naturally shy or less likely to raise their hand when they have a question or answer. It gives students who need more time to process, or who think better by writing things down, a way to contribute to full-class discussion that is better suited to them. For those students who shine when called on, they still have a chance to contribute their best voice when we bring the discussion to the board.

Through Pear Deck's teacher dashboard, I can see how students are responding in real-time to monitor individual needs at the same time I am looking at the overall class analytics. Through the projector view, I can display these responses on the board. If I am asking a multiple-choice or number-type question, we can review the breakdown of answers as a class. If most of the class chose an incorrect multiple-choice answer, this can be a wonderful opportunity to talk about why so many students chose the wrong solution. And since each student has responded to the question on their own device, the answers displayed, though shared anonymously, are representative of the voice of all students in the classroom.

With Pear Deck, you have an instantaneous breakdown of responses. That information drives whether I take a moment to go over the question at hand as a class, or if I wait to individually sit down with students who answered incorrectly. With the short-answer-type questions, I have the chance to display the work of each student in my classroom on the board so that we can discuss these collective answers and dive deeper into topics and connections. Since I can hide student names when projecting the answers submitted, I am able to provide a safe space for each student to honestly respond without worrying about how their peers might perceive their viewpoint or approach to a problem.

When I use Pear Deck in Student-Paced Mode, students can move through the deck at a pace that best fits their needs. This allows me to ask a question and give each student the space and time to actively engage with the questions on their own device. We often pressure students into quickly responding, or we can be fast to assume that a student who is responding slowly does not know the material as well as a peer who immediately knows what to do. With Pear Deck's Student-Paced Mode, we lessen the risk of doing this. Because the teacher dashboard allows me to see students working in real-time, I can instantly identify if a student is just progressing slowly or if they are stuck and might need some help. I use the information I am seeing in the dashboard to focus my attention and know what student, or group of students, needs my energy. I can do all this without having to peek over a student's shoulder, trying to guess what they are writing on their paper. This happens organically while everyone in the class is actively engaged in a task, so it's not obvious I am going over to any specific students who are struggling or need help. I am casually walking around, checking in while students work, but I know which students need a little extra attention without them having to ask.

As a math teacher, one of my favorite Pear Deck features is the drawing type question. I have a class set of Wacom tablets. Students plug the Wacoms into their laptops and then are free to handwrite their responses to questions as they would on a piece of paper. The real-time feedback provided through the Pear Deck teacher dashboard is particularly powerful; it enables me to get a glimpse into *how* they are approaching and working through problems. As a math teacher, it is far more important for me to see a student's process than their final answer.

After students have had a chance to respond, I take back control of navigation so that we can discuss answers as a whole class. For students who are more vocal, their best work might be that moment we bring the conversation to the board to talk about the various answers. But Pear Deck levels the playing field by also providing an outlet for students who need time to process and type out their thoughts, or who are naturally quieter.

Students "drawing" on a Pear Deck
slide using a Wacom tablet

It's important to understand that using Pear Deck is not about having students simply hide behind their laptops, typing their thoughts. Pear Deck is a platform that allows teachers to create a safe space for *all* students to contribute. And as we look at the responses of the class, it's not just about highlighting the correct answers. In fact, sometimes it is more important to break down the incorrect ones and target where in the solution process the error occurred. I believe that when students make mistakes, we—as teachers—need to ask why. It is not about putting the blame on anybody, but when a student fails to understand material covered in class, it begs the question: *Why?*

How can we help students learn from mistakes? And how can we transform those errors into learning experiences for the whole class? There is great power in analyzing incorrect answers. The problem is that I am not willing to put a student on the spot for a failed attempt.

> *Mistakes grow your brain.*
> —Jo Boaler

Since I am able to display student work without a name attached to that response, I feel free to use these answers as the basis for discussion instead of putting my own correct solution up on the board and working from there. We then talk about which answers are correct and dissect the incorrect ones, tackling where the student's thinking went wrong and helping them identify and explain mistakes. Not only does the whole class benefit from this analysis, but the student who made the error has an opportunity to see where his approach went wrong.

Note: Of course, my students should not feel ashamed of incorrect answers, and I try my best to stress how important mistakes are in the learning process. Still, calling out students when they are incorrect in front of the whole class is something I am uncomfortable doing. My hope is that running class as I do, with the anonymity Pear Deck provides, will help everyone in my classroom see how many mistakes we all make; and hopefully that knowledge will help them feel less fearful of making errors themselves. I guess it's just something I wish a teacher would have helped me work through.

With Pear Deck, all students can truly participate. It's not about having students come up to the board one at a time to talk about their work. We can display all responses and discuss what the *class* is saying. It is key that the teacher create this sense of class community in how they integrate the technology and structure the

Pear Deck so that there is time for typing but also time for talking. In this way, we are no longer just discussing one student's answer. We're discussing the whole class's results.

> In this way, we are no longer just discussing one student's answer. We're discussing the whole class's results.

At the conclusion of an activity, with Pear Deck's Takeaways, each student receives a copy of each of the slides with their answers in a Google Doc. This Google Doc is automatically shared between just the teacher and the student. Teachers can choose to open the Google Doc after class to leave students comments. Or teachers can ask students to go back to the Google Doc to correct, summarize, and reflect. My typical workflow is to ask students to turn in reflections on their Takeaways prior to each assessment, as in the example below. Having students rework their warm-ups and make connections between the various activities is a powerful exercise in helping students understand the big picture. Also, reflecting on prior work is a powerful way to help students review what they've learned. Pear Deck's Takeaways makes creating this task seamless.

At the end of the day, Pear Deck is all about moving the focus of a presentation from the teacher to the student. Each and every student in my classroom is engaged in the conversation and required to participate. As the teacher, I am equipped with powerful analytics, which give me a sense of class trends and indicators of individual students who are struggling. That instantaneous breakdown of responses that Pear Deck provides drives the direction of class and the focus of conversation so that class can be about what students actually need versus what I think we need to get through. It's no longer about calling one student up to the board to have an active classroom. With Pear Deck, each student is given control, and we can discuss what the whole class has to say. That level of engagement and personalization is what has taken my classroom to a whole new level.

Part 1 - Summary

Use this space to summarize your thoughts on the lesson

I now better understand the limit definition of a derivative, both visually and algebraically. I can see that as h->0 means we are pulling those two points close together and how the secant line approaches the tangent line. And I can now recognize that the limit formula can represent the derivative of a function at a point.

Part 2 - Responses

Slide 1 - Drawing	Your Response
Extension: 2.4-2.5 Evaluate: $\lim_{x \to \infty} \frac{e^x+5}{10+e^x}$	

Use this space for notes:

Remember to look at the graph of e^x to determine end behavior at positive vs negative infinity.

Slide 2 - Drawing	Your Response
Extension: 2.4-2.5 Evaluate: $\lim_{x \to -\infty} \frac{e^x+5}{10+e^x}$	

Sample: Page from a Pear Deck Takeaway Google Doc

The Perfect Pairing: Zoom + Pear Deck

Whether in my flipped classroom or my virtual "face-to-face" with my Online AP Calculus AB students via our weekly Zoom sessions, thoughtfully engaging students is a priority. Particularly in a setting where I only see my online students once per week, the last thing I want is to just be talking *at* them for that precious hour we have together.

To engage students in virtual class Zoom sessions, I use Pear Deck. I create a Pear Deck ahead of time that includes an introductory activity, some problems we will work together, and discussion questions to help us develop deeper understandings, etc. Students log into Zoom at our scheduled time and sign into the Pear Deck I have linked them to. I sign into the same Pear Deck I assign students—as a teacher in one tab and as a student in another.[3] I respond to the questions alongside my students so that we can compare all responses, mine included. The first couple slides are typically the warm-up activity that students engage with at their own pace. We then get into problem-solving, which are mainly Pear Deck drawing type questions. Because students all have Wacom Intuos tablets, they can write freely on the Pear Deck. What's amazing is that I see them writing in real time through the teacher dashboard, even though we are all in different physical places. Since I don't see students working problems in the classroom, seeing them work through the problems during this session gives me incredibly valuable feedback and insight into their understandings.

After several minutes of the introductory activity, I switch off the Student-Paced Mode so that I can control the navigation through the Pear Deck slides and we can all be in-sync. We begin by

---

3 In Pear Deck, you can be logged into Pear Deck as a teacher and also use the join code to log in as a student using the same Google account, at the same time.

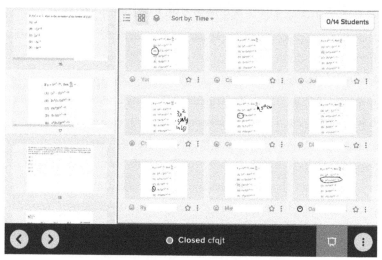

Pear Deck Teacher Dashboard View with
Drawing Updating in Real Time

reviewing student responses to the warm-up and talking about any corrections or clarifications needed. We continue to move through the Pear Deck, with each student writing independently on their own device. In Zoom, I can do a screenshare to show what I am writing or to display student work (remember, I am also logged into the Pear Deck as a student so I can draw on the slides using Pear Deck's drawing tools in the same way students can). There are moments where I use the Pear Deck for instruction and other times when I have students solve problems, and then we review and talk about those answers as a class. (If you are interested in seeing a short clip from a Zoom session in action, check out the resources page of my website at techiemusings.com/techwithheart.)

At the conclusion of the Zoom, each student gets a copy of the work they did in Pear Deck when I publish the "Takeaways," and I also share the work that I have done with them by sharing my own filled-out Pear Deck Takeaway for students to study from.

The Must-Have Tools in my Flipped Classroom

I have focused so much on tools in this section. While the tools themselves did not change my classroom, the potential to get such detailed information on how students process material and the immediacy of feedback has transformed how I teach. I've thoughtfully selected each tool for a reason, I ask questions that help me get insight into what's on a student's mind, and I carefully read each response so that my students know I care about them as a person.

My flipped classroom has evolved and continues to transform as tech tools provide new and exciting ways to get insight into students' needs. These tools allow me to provide a level of personalization and customization that simply was not possible less than five years ago. But it's not so much about the tools as it is about the *why*. Technology has allowed me to get to know my students as individuals, deepen the relationships I can build, hear from each and every student in my classroom, and be the most efficient teacher I can be.

Tools that help me achieve this goal are what I would call essential in my flipped classroom—and teaching in general. These are some of the tools I've used:

To Engage Students	On the Creation End
• Pear Deck	• Camtasia
• Edpuzzle	• Wacom tablet
• Flipgrid	• YouTube

You can find direct links to these tools on my website at techiemusings.com/techwithheart.

Learning Online Does Not Mean Learning in Isolation

My first year teaching Online AP Calculus AB was one of the most incredible learning experiences I've had. It pushed me to creatively reimagine my classroom. It forced me to think deeply about why I had set up certain practices in my face-to-face classroom and how important it was to maintain this dynamic in my online class. It required me to look deeply into a variety of tech tools to creatively reimagine how I might be able to "hack" them to fulfill my needs. From creating a differentiated learning experience for each student in the class to teaching juniors and seniors to be truly resourceful and independent to creating an inspired, connected classroom of online learners and continuing to get to know my students on a deeply personal level, developing my online class has taken my teaching practice to the next level.

One of my biggest goals in designing the class was to keep the collaboration and personalization alive in an online environment! Making the course feel connected—both student-to-student and teacher-to-student—was one of my top priorities. I wanted to ensure that my students felt they were part of a class community, working together to build and strengthen understanding, and strongly connected to me, their teacher. One easy solution was to include assignments each week that required teamwork. Learning online does not mean learning in isolation; in fact, some of the most powerful learning moments happen when students help and explain concepts to one another. As a teacher, the thing I value most is getting to know my students as individuals. It's not just about teaching them math—it's about learning their strengths and weaknesses so I can help them maximize success, build confidence, and, most of all, enjoy the process of learning!

With these goals in mind, I carefully selected tech tools to help me achieve my goals. This course was not going to run without the

> Learning online does not mean learning in isolation; in fact, some of the most powerful learning moments happen when students help and explain concepts to one another.

help of technology, after all. I put a lot of thought into the tools I chose, and I wanted to be sure to communicate my "why" to help students understand course goals. And, as I had learned in my flipped classroom, I was sure to communicate this message to parents as well, by sending home a detailed newsletter. (You can check out the newsletter on the resources page of my website at techiemusings.com/techwithheart if you are interested.)

To me, ensuring that both students and parents understand the class format and expectations, and the exciting opportunities for communication and reflection that students would have in the online environment, was critical in building trust from the start. I am honest with my students in explaining my *why*, and I also provide them opportunities to give me feedback and ideas. We build a strong level of trust and respect, and that, to me, is the key.

I won't go into the details of the newsletter here, as most of the tools are discussed elsewhere in the book. But the one tool I have not talked much about, and which has been vital in our communication, is Slack.

I rely on Slack to have real-time conversations.

What is Slack:[4] It's real-time messaging, archiving, and searching for modern teams.

How we use Slack: Slack enables students to problem-solve collaboratively (like they might text message a friend for

---

4 Per Slack's terms of service, all users must be over sixteen years of age to use, which my students are.

homework help), is a way for them to ask questions (privately to me and publicly to the class), and allows opportunity to provide help to their classmates.

Slack has been an incredibly effective communication tool for us. We all have the Slack app on our phones and notifications set up on our computers. I set up a public channel for each chapter so that we can organize chapter-specific questions. And I also have a private feedback channel for each student. The private feedback channel is a way for me to write students' individual corrections based on their homework submissions and also a place for them to ask me any private questions. My students *love* Slack and the instant communication we can maintain.

One thing I was worried about, initially, was that it would be difficult to emote compassion, energy, and excitement in the online environment since we often do that with facial expressions, hand gestures, and voice intonation. One strategy is that I give video and voice feedback, and also often use a 🙂 and am sure to follow-up with a ❗ in our Slack communication channel. I suppose it's my way of bringing that upbeat energy to the online environment that I try to always bring into the classroom. This has been working well overall. It's a careful balance—I want to maintain the expectation that students write in full sentences with proper spelling and grammar. But I always want them to sense when I'm being lighthearted or just giving them a dose of encouragement. And I want to feel the same from my students. Based on course feedback, I would say things are working well:

> "I really enjoyed the freedom and responsibility the course provided me. I also thought that, by being online, I had more time to focus on what I needed to. I also thought the teacher was very enthusiastic and always helpful whenever help was needed, pretty much regardless of the time of day."

> "I really enjoy the liberty I have with Slack when I can study and work on my work. I love love love the Slack channel because it provides a great outlet for me to get my questions answered."

Teaching, for me, is all about being empathetic and aware that how students (and parents) *feel* can significantly impact performance. Taking the time to nurture positive relationships and trust upfront pays off ten-fold.

Student Feedback at the End of My First Year Teaching Online AP Calculus AB

"I don't know why I love it [Online AP Calculus], but I tell everyone it's my favorite class. For the first time it's made me really, really enjoy math."

"What I've enjoyed most has been the freedom in the style of course. It suits me and allows me to work in the most focused environment for myself."

"You may think since it's an online class that you're not going to be connected as much with other people in the class or with the teacher. But you actually are always connected through things like Slack. And each week, we have a Google Hangout where we interact with the other students."

"[This course has] helped me build skills to be independent and also to reach out and ask questions when I don't understand something. Previously, especially in math, I wouldn't want to ask questions if I didn't understand something because I would be embarrassed. But that does not happen at all in this class. I ask questions whenever I need and it's really great."

"I am so unbelievably happy that I chose the online course. You can message your teacher on Slack, and she'll get back to you so quickly, whereas I know a lot of teachers take a while when it comes to responding to emails. I also really like the freedom of the course. [You can choose] whether you want to do your work all at once early or if you want to do it later. And I just think it was one of the best classes that I ever chose to take, and if I were to choose again, I would definitely choose to do online. It was awesome."

STUDENTS HELPING BEYOND THE CLASSROOM

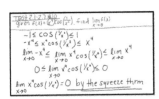

No better way to LEARN than through TEACHING

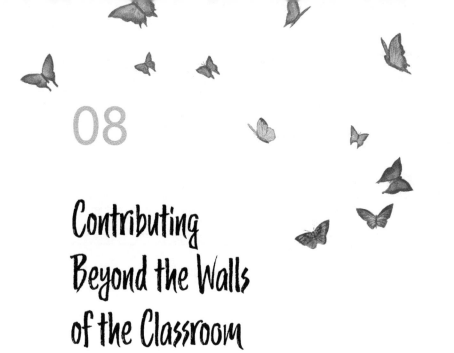

08

Contributing Beyond the Walls of the Classroom

*Teachers need to stop saying, "Hand it in,"
and start saying, "Publish it," instead.*

—Alan November

The power of having a global voice and audience really struck me when I started making my flipped classroom videos. The process of creating such a large resource of free, publicly available videos online for the world to see has allowed me to experience the wonder of having my voice reach way beyond my immediate classroom. Math, being a truly global language, has allowed students from around the world to learn from my videos. The internet is an amazing place, and students turn to YouTube or an internet search immediately when they are looking to learn something new.

Abbas Akbar commented on your video

5.2 - The Definite Integral

Abbas Akbar

Starting my second Calculus course. Got an A for my last Calc class in the fall using your videos, I don't know where I would be without these. Thank you SO so much, you are unbelievably helpful and deserve an award! :)

has sent you a message

You can reply to this message by visiting your inbox.

To:Stacey Roshan

I just wanted to say thank you so much for all of your math videos! They have really helped me understand and do well on tests. My parents can't afford a tutor and so your videos were life savors! Thank you so so so much!

New comment on your video
8.6 - Solve Rational Expressions

t m

Ms. Roshan, I must say that you are THE BEST algebra teacher I have ever come across. I really appreciate your videos, because of them I aced my last algebra 2 test! Please continue to make more

New comment on your video
7.4 - Evaluate Logarithms and Graph Logarithmic Functions

TryHardPilot

u are the best no doubt about it, my whole class watch your videos, tomorrow is my midterm exam and u literally saved my life, i had troubles graphing logarithms but now its easy thanks to you

New comment on your video
8.4 - Multiply and Divide Rational Functions

jessy chan
Yet again saving grades out here 😄 I failed my last quiz for not coming over to your channel and checking out the video for it

Akash Chaudhari
Your videos help so much!!! Please do not stop them EVER!!! I absolutely have no clue to what my teacher does in class so I usually almost everyday come home and just watch your video on that lesson and BAM just like that is makes sense!! Otherwise this is me in my class ....
Anyway your doing a great job and helping so many students learn how to actually do their homework instead of just copying so keep it up!!!!! :)))

Reply   View all comments

Akanksha Bhatt
You are just great!!! I mean your videos have brought me from being a B student to an A student
Ur awesome!!!

Reply   View all comments

New comment on your video
7.7 - Write and Apply Exponential and Power Functions

MsAlaskanGirl907
I think you're the first person to make math fun for me since 3rd grade. Thank you!!

111

I have received some of the most amazing thank you notes from students resourceful enough to spend the extra time finding and studying the videos I post to YouTube.

Several years back, I considered how I might be able to inspire my students to experience the power of contributing to and getting feedback from a larger, authentic audience. In fact, I decided to make it a priority in my classroom. Now, part of my course syllabus specifies that, beyond contributing to discussions and staying on task, a major component of class is helping others work through challenges, near and far.

It's amazing what technology can do to help us connect our students to a global and authentic audience. Having students chat about math and contribute to solution forums requires them to verbalize their math thought process and dive deeper into connecting concepts. Not only does this do wonders for solidifying concepts and helping them understand the *why* behind their solution, I think it helps students think differently about math class. If you ask a student about their math homework and the first things they mention are the mountains of worksheets they are assigned each unit, well, it's no wonder those students dread doing that work! Yes, repetition and practice are necessary in math class; but worksheets aren't the only solution. If we get students talking about their math work and give them more chances to chat out their solution process, we can help them grasp complex concepts more deeply.

For years now, I've had my students post math solutions to Socratic.org, which is a forum where students can go to ask or answer questions for a variety of academic disciplines.[1] Several times each trimester, I required students to post a math solution

---

1 Unfortunately, Socratic has recently discontinued this service and is now a purely mobile app for students to get homework help. I'm sure I'll find a similar solution soon, but at the moment, I don't have an alternative platform to suggest.

to Socratic. I also encouraged them to use the forum beyond the requirements of the class to show an individual interest and effort to go above and beyond. I think it's so important to have students contributing to a global, authentic audience, and Socratic.org was a great forum for this in my calculus classroom. This exercise also emphasized process over just the final answer and really forced students to be able to verbalize each part of their solution. In math, we require students to "show all work," which is one way for students to document how they're thinking through a problem. But these solution posts take the level of detail required to the next level to help students become more adept at fluently describing the *why* behind their math logic.

Additionally, I ask students to create mini video lessons of their own. As you've read in previous sections, we use Flipgrid to simplify the process of creating quick video explanations. My students this year are adding to Flipgrid topics I started with students I've taught over the past two years. In this way, my current students can learn from a wider library of student-created content. These student-created solutions might not be as "perfect" as the instructional videos we make as teachers, but they have a level of empathy that we cannot possibly recreate. Students tend to get stuck in similar areas and, because they are learning together, there is a certain level of compassion and understanding that a student-to-student explanation can provide that can't be matched by the teacher. Instead of needing the "expert teacher" to re-explain the topic, this exercise allows for powerful peer-to-peer learning.

Right now, our math Flipgrid discussions have not reached students outside of our school. I have assignments planned for the spring, however, that will be public,[2] so I can team up with other

---

2 Flipgrid actually has a CoPilots sharing option so that teachers can team up to co-create and co-moderate grids.

AP Calculus AB teachers to expand our reach and allow my students to learn from and teach students across the United States.

The process of creating these responses in Socratic and Flipgrid, whether they are public to just our class or to a global audience, requires students to go beyond simply showing the computation used in arriving at an answer and think through how they would like an answer to be explained to them. I believe that students reinforce their learning and gain deeper insight into material by teaching others, and this is the main goal I am working to achieve. By weaving these activities into my classroom from the beginning of the year, I have noticed that students are naturally comfortable with the idea of "fully justifying" their solution by the time we get to the AP exam. Before we integrated these activities, this was not the case for my students.

There are many clear benefits to integrating this type of teaching into the classroom. First, we're building a set of study resources specifically tailored to our classwork. We're also building a record of each student's progress throughout the year, which is powerful to look back on and makes a great addition to a student's ePortfolio (more on that in the next section, Documenting Growth and Connecting Knowledge). Perhaps most importantly, though, I believe that having students explain their problem-solving process at this level of detail is critical to helping them build their analytical and verbal math skills—a task that's often overlooked in mathematics pedagogy. And because students are creating this work digitally, they can easily share their work with a public, global audience. As I mentioned at the opening of this chapter, an internet search is often our first stop when we have a question. I can't imagine a better way to empower my students and share the importance of generously helping others!

09

The Power of Reflection and Metacognition

I used to think great teachers inspire you. Now I think I had it wrong. Good teachers inspire you; great teachers show you how to inspire yourself every day of your life. They don't show you their magic. They show you how to make magic of your own.

—Alfred Doblin

A big area of growth in my teaching has been building in regular opportunities for students to reflect, document improvement, and engage in the metacognitive process of thinking about their own thinking.

Creating Flipgrid Private Channels for Questions and Reflections in Online AP Calculus

When I began teaching Online AP Calculus, I knew that Flipgrid was going to be a lifesaver and critical tool in helping me hear my students "talk." One of the things I value most about being a teacher is having the opportunity to enjoy each student's personality and to get to know each one as an individual (and for them to feel this same connection with me).

In year two of teaching Online AP Calculus AB, I wanted to do more with Flipgrid to set up an easy communication channel with students. In year one of teaching in the purely online format, I focused a lot of energy on finding ways for the class to collaboratively work through problems—both orally (using Google Hangouts and Zoom) and through written chat (using Slack). In my second year, I wanted to add in more private communication opportunities between me and the student. In year one, my main way of communicating one-on-one with students was through Slack, which meant typed text or handwritten feedback. Sometimes, I would include a video response to a question, but students never sent me video messages.

One thing I wanted to work on in year two was allowing more differentiation in our private communication. Video can be powerful, and sometimes it is more effective to talk things out than to type them. Also, things can get lost in translation when typing, especially when it comes to being able to read emotions and other cues that might show up when you see a person versus when they send written communication.

So I decided to set up a private Flipgrid channel between me and each student. I'll explain how I've set this up in the section titled "The Setup." But to begin, for each student, I create two private topics for them:

1: Questions Flipgrid

This is a private video discussion board between the student and me because sometimes it is easier to talk out a question than to type it. The student is instructed to add a video response to this Flipgrid anytime they want to ask a question or discuss an issue. Again, this is a private communication channel between me and the student, so they can talk honestly about questions or concerns.

2: Reflections Flipgrid

This is another private video discussion board between the student and me. Students are instructed to use this space to talk about things they're doing well, areas they are working to improve, problems they've identified, and general reflections. I also ask that they take a moment to talk about their growth in this class (how they've deepened their understandings, new connections they've made, etc.). I think it's important to remind them to take note of something they are proud of because it is easy to get swept away in thinking about all the many ways they could be improving. Building in moments for reflection on a consistent basis is a big goal of mine. I will elaborate more on specific prompts I used for these activities in the next section.

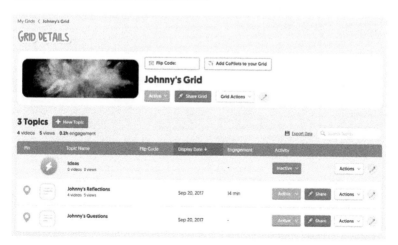

The Setup

To set things up, I created a separate grid for each student, as I wanted this to be a private communication between the student and me. The only way to make things private in Flipgrid is to password protect the grid. Password protection is a grid-level setting (not a topic-level setting), so I needed to create a grid for each student.

Within each grid, I set up two topics.

1. Questions Grid

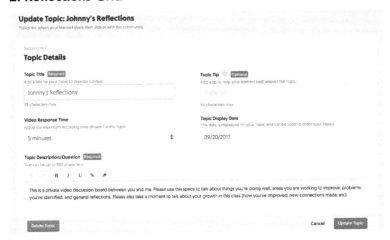

2. Reflections Grid

Flipgrid provides a simple way for students to send me a video without having to upload any files. And because of the way that Flipgrid is set up, it is a natural dialogue between me and the student. The Reflections Flipgrid was a powerful way for students to document progress throughout the year. However, maybe more importantly, it really helped build stronger relationships with my students as I learned about their goals and interest beyond the math classroom.

Reflections to Process Feedback and to Learn from Fails

As I continued to think on the topic of reflections, I thought about its role in my own growth. Personally, I am constantly reflecting on what I've done, brainstorming how I will make refinements, and planning towards those goals. One of the most powerful exercises, for me, was beginning my blog, techiemusings.com. I started blogging as a way to get my thoughts out "on paper" and to have one spot where I could refer back to things I had researched, learned, and thought about. But as I continued blogging, I found that it provided this amazing way to connect with others—a way for me to share my ideas with the world and get feedback and ideas for improvement. And I turned to other people's blogs to inspire me. I will regularly find an idea that someone else has tried and then "remix" that assignment to meet the needs of my class and my students. Now that I've blogged about so many assignments I've run and shifts to my classroom I've worked hard to make, I continue to look back at old posts as I refine my classroom and build. I love comparing my posts from year to year to see the growth I've made and help bring attention to areas that still need work. It's fun to look for trends in my writing and see how these align with my formal professional goals. Writing helps keep me focused, centered, and pushing forward with clear vision.

As I thought about the power of reflection in my teaching, I asked myself how I could incorporate similar exercises into my classroom. In the past year, I have worked to incorporate general reflection into classwork on a regular basis.

One way I do this is by asking students to do a biweekly task where they summarize three main takeaways from my feedback on their assignments. Sometimes I ask students to write or type this out, and other times I ask them to create a Flipgrid response and chat things out to the camera. I enjoy seeing students respond in multiple formats, and some students certainly feel more comfortable with one format over the other—which is all the more reason to switch things up.

The goal of this assignment is multi-fold. Of course, by asking students to reflect on my feedback, I am able to check that they have actually read my annotations. But more importantly, by asking them to summarize their main takeaways, they are being required to synthesize my comments, look for patterns and trends, and think about the work they have done over the course of the week. This also gives me a chance to see how students are taking in my feedback. Particularly when they are responding via Flipgrid, I get a clear sense of how they are processing my notes, whether they are picking up on big themes or getting lost in the minutiae, and if they are left feeling more confident or still feeling confused or frustrated.

Beyond the feedback reflections, I also do general reflections with students once or twice a month. They are instructed to give themselves five minutes to reflect and write (or record) on the prompts that I outline below. If the assignment is written, they do not need to write in full sentences. They know that this is not meant to be a formal, polished presentation but rather a quick goal setting and reflection activity.

You can find a direct link to each of these Flipgrid prompts, which you can copy and modify for your own needs, on the resources page of my website at techiemusings.com/techwithheart.

Talk about a Failure

General Reflection

- What's a major fail you had this week? This does not have to be related to class.
- How did your initial approach to the problem/situation lead you astray?
- How has your approach to the problem/situation changed now? How has your thinking shifted?
- What is one thing you can take away as a lesson learned from this "fail"? How can you turn this into a future "win"?

Calculus Specific

- What question did you royally mess up on during your first attempt?
- How did your initial approach to the problem lead you astray?
- How has your approach to the problem changed now? How has your thinking shifted?
- What is one thing you can take away as a lesson learned from this "fail"? How can you turn this into a future "win"?

Talk about a Win

General Reflection

- What's a major win you had this week?

- How did your initial approach to the problem/situation lead to your success?
- What is one thing you can take away as a lesson learned from this "win"? How can you apply this lesson to help you find future successes?

Calculus Specific

- What question did you totally crush this week?
- How did your approach to the problem lead you to success?
- What is one thing you can take away as a lesson learned from this "win"? How can you apply this process to help you find future successes?

I enjoy asking the general reflection questions, particularly in my online class, to help me gain a more holistic relationship with the student. Their responses help me get a sense of the student beyond just the math classroom. Often, their wins are something completely outside of academics (i.e., catching a fish, making a goal in a game, picking up a sibling). But most importantly, I hope that by repeating this activity throughout the year, using the same format, my students will begin naturally reflecting on wins and fails in their life and use the prompts I have given them to help them bounce back from their "fails" and to learn from their "wins." I hope, also, that some students will see the value of these activities for their own self-improvement and continue the practice of regular reflection.

Documenting Growth and Connecting Knowledge

In my AP Calculus course, I wanted students to look back on past work and connect it to new knowledge. Reflection is key to learning, and I wanted to create a project to help students strengthen their understanding of the relationships between "old" and "new" material. I wanted students to go back to material we had done in early chapters and reflect on how their understanding of these problems had evolved and grown.

I decided to structure a project to focus on having students:

- reflect on new connections formed
- document how their understandings have grown
- capture strategies to maximize their learning

I asked students to use Sutori, a web tool that allows students to tell a story in a linear, visually appealing format (looks like a linear timeline) to document this work. Sutori easily allows students to capture artifacts they want to highlight—whether it be embedded content (i.e., Flipgrid videos), audio recordings, images, or text. In addition to including the elements they chose to highlight, they use text captions to describe why they chose that piece of work. These text captions were an important part of having students capture their reflective process.

AP Calculus Trimester 1 Project
By Eshan

I choose to do a limit problem because throughout the year we have learned multiple different methods of finding tangent lines, instantaneous rates of change, and velocity equations.

Share   Comment

On my original attempt at this problem, I had not yet learned about how to find a derivative of a function nor what a derivative even was. At this time of the year, we had only learned this one method of finding the instantaneous rate of change. This method was very straightforward at the time which I used to my advantage because it was easy to practice and drill similar problems to become very efficient via this method of finding the derivative of the function.

Share   Comment

During the time of this year, I had not really understood what the f'(x) really meant and what the equation really told us. Now, I know that the f'(x) equation gives us information about the direction of the graph, where the graph is increasing and decreasing, the extremas of the graph, and helps us find the critical numbers of the graph. This graph can also be used in real world applications such as using the MVT to find people who are speeding.

Share   Comment

Quiz   ✐ Edit

Some New Differentiation Rules

Product Rule

$$\frac{d}{dx}\left[f(x)g(x)\right] = f(x)g'(x) + g(x)f'(x)$$

Quotient Rule

Original Attempt at the Problem

Share   Comment

How I would do this question now with what I have learned using product and/or quotient rule.

Share   Comment

Student Project: Sample Reflection Element
from Trimester 1 Project

Project Purpose, Goals, and Intended Outcomes

This project forced students to not only look back at old work but to be selective about what they chose and why they chose it. They needed to think deeply about their initial approach to the problem and think through the results:

- What knowledge had not yet been gained when completing this task initially that you now have? How has this information taken your understanding to a new level?
- If you were to redo this problem now, would you use the same approach? Or have we learned something new that would allow you to come up with a more elegant or simpler solution?
- If you solved the problem algebraically, can you represent your solution graphically now, or vice versa? How do you interpret each to represent the same solution?

Beyond capturing individual problems, students were also asked to do a detailed reflection and goal setting:

- What did you do well? How will you ensure that you continue to make a habit of this?
- What could use improvement? What action steps will you take to boost future outcomes?
- What strategies have you learned that work well for you as a learner? How can you apply this to your future studies?

Student Project: Goals and Reflections Section
with Audio and Video Elements

What's Next

After students received detailed feedback from me on their projects, they made corrections to their work. In Sutori, everything is auto-saved and auto-shared with me (since I have set up a Sutori class), so there is no passing back and forth of information, which is great. After students made revisions, we shared these Sutori projects as a class. Students were then asked to review the work of one or two other classmates, engage with the content on that page, and also write up a reflective statement on what they learned by reviewing their peer's project.

Making It Stick

As all our brain-based research says, learning sticks when students connect what they are learning to their own prior knowledge. That is the main goal of this project—to help students look back on past work and connect it to new knowledge. Reflection is key to learning, and this project provides students the opportunity to develop deeper connections between the chapters we have studied. This exercise is also all about helping students learn how to learn.

> *When you practice elaboration, there's no known limit to how much you can learn. Elaboration is the process of giving new material meaning by expressing it in your own words and connecting it with what you already know. The more you can explain about the way your new learning relates to your prior knowledge, the stronger your grasp of the new learning will be, and the more connections you create that will help you remember it later.*
>
> —Peter C. Brown, *Make It Stick*

In addition to the fact that students learn a lot in compiling the work they choose to showcase and reflecting on that work, I think this project helps students gain a new level of confidence in completing this project. They have come a long way in their learning since the start of the year, and this project allows them to highlight and "see" this growth.

Using Pear Deck with Embedded Flipgrid Question to Develop Deeper Connections

As I've worked to improve my lesson design and layer in metacognition, I have looked to edtech, once again, to help me come up with my solution. One such activity that I've developed uses Pear Deck to create student-paced activities with questions that ramp up in difficulty to help students discover new ideas and promote higher-order thinking skills. Since I find that having students chat their ideas out in these discovery-based activities is usually most effective, I looked to Flipgrid to assist in reaching this goal. And then I discovered how easy it is to embed a Flipgrid topic into a Pear Deck using a "web slide," so this idea fully came to life.

One of the biggest problems I see as a math teacher is when students try to "memorize" how to do problems. I'll see them create elaborate note sheets listing the procedural "steps" they should take to solve a variety of question types. The problem here is that, when presented with some slight variation to the problems they are used to, they panic because they think they're seeing some new question type. This is particularly evident when students are asked to do word problems and applications (thus the bad rap associated with these question types). In my opinion, there is no place for memorization in math class. The problem with memorizing very procedural steps is that students are no longer breaking down the question and thinking through what is given, what is missing, and what is the goal. Instead, what's most important is that we help students understand the process of deeply analyzing problems—writing down what they know, piecing together the information they have, and being unafraid to just "play." Of course, this takes longer and is more challenging than teaching to the test.

To help students get comfortable with this type of process, I decided to create a series of Pear Deck + Flipgrid activities in a similar format. If the topic was optimization, for instance, then I might concentrate on a theme, questions involving a box with an open top, then ask a series of questions related to this box. (You can find a direct link to the Pear Deck activity on the resources page of my website at techiemusings.com/techwithheart.) Let's start with three simple optimization questions related to this box:

- Maximize the volume of the box.
- Minimize the material used to build the box.
- Minimize the cost of constructing the box.

The goal here is to help students see that, even though all of these questions involve optimization with an open top box, the approach is dependent on what is being asked, not the "question type."

To help students understand how to think through the problem, I asked them the same series of questions for each maximization/minimization problem:

- Draw a picture; label what's given and what you're trying to find.
- Write out what you're trying to optimize and determine what formula will represent that.
- What other information does the question provide that might help you solve this question? What type of formula can you come up with to represent this information?
- In Flipgrid, talk out your strategy for tackling this problem.

The reason I like doing this activity in Pear Deck is that students can easily draw, write, type, and talk to their webcam (via the embedded Flipgrid) without having to move between tools.

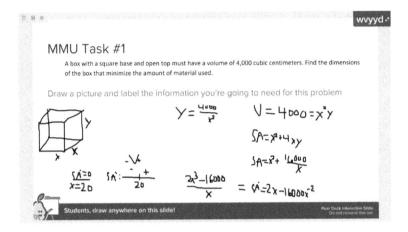

After responding to all these pre-tasks, I finally ask students to solve the problem. Within the Pear Deck, I also layered in some other reflection questions, such as the following:

- What if, instead of creating a box with an open top, you included the top in the construction? What would change? How would your equations change to reflect this?
- Why do you think I created this assignment for you? What is the relationship between the questions asked in this activity?
- What did this exercise help clarify?

By the end of this activity, my hope is that optimization problems will seem less intimidating for my students. Through the prompts I've included in Pear Deck, and by embedding reflection questions along the way, students are required to give their own meaning to each step. The process allows students to gain a deeper understanding of how to visualize and model a broad range of scenarios. It helps them realize the similarities and differences in approaching several question types and gives them a framework for solving other questions. Most importantly, this activity helps students become more aware of their own thinking process, while simultaneously giving me powerful insight into that thought process as well. The better insight we can get into how our students are thinking, the deeper we can connect with them and understand their needs.

What content do I need to deliver today?

How do I best address the questions that students are actually struggling with?

10

Change Leads to Innovation

A teacher plants the seeds of knowledge, sprinkles them with love, and patiently nurtures their growth to produce tomorrow's dreams.

—Unknown

I firmly believe that through changes and challenging the way things have always been done, we grow as teachers. At the same time, conversations about the "side effects" and impact of these changes are equally important. I'll start by saying that when I was first asked to teach a purely online course, I was nervous and not sure that I was excited about the idea. Three years later, I can say that teaching online has been one of the biggest and best growth opportunities for me. I can't say that I enjoy teaching it in the same way I enjoy my face-to-face teaching, but it's a different challenge and a wonderful one. We are all naturally fearful of big shifts in how we do things, but the way I see it, if we can have conversations as we roll out change and continue to communicate intentions, these changes lead to very positive growth.

Teaching a purely online course has forced me to be creative and intentional in ways that the face-to-face environment doesn't require. I have enjoyed the challenge and opportunity to grow. It has helped me become a more reflective educator, and building a community of learners has taken on some new meaning.

But at the end of the day, whether I am teaching online or face-to-face, my biggest goals remain constant. I want to spark joy in my students and help them gain confidence in their math aptitude. I want to create a strong class community and let every student know that I care for them as an individual. I want to be there to listen to my students, have an awareness of their needs, and make them feel supported. I want to create an awesome experience for my students, where they feel challenged but capable of achieving success beyond what they have ever accomplished in math class. I want to push my students and help them develop habits that will allow them to achieve a healthy balance in life.

In conclusion, I want to thank you for this chance to take you through my journey. This was a scary book to write for a variety of reasons: 1) I have never talked about my personal struggles publicly, and rarely even privately; and 2) I never want to sound like an expert who runs this perfect classroom and has it all figured out. But my fears were outweighed by the thought that my story might help a fellow teacher, administrator, or even a parent gain a new perspective in dealing with a child who needs help—whether that struggle is externally visible or not. I look forward to continuing to become a better teacher and learning better self-care. I know that I can be a powerful model to my students, and only by taking a dose of my own advice will I be able to effect any change in others.

If we **EMPOWER** students with the resources they need and **COACH** them through the process of using these tools, then students can take **OWNERSHIP** for their learning. And that's where the **MAGIC** happens.

Bibliography

CHAPTER 1

Roshan, Stacey. "The Best Way to Reach Each Student? Private School Math Teacher Flips Learning." The Daily Riff, March 25, 2012. thedailyriff.com/articles/the-best-way-to-reach-each-student-private-school-flips-learning-547.php.

Schaffhauser, Diana. "The Backwards Class." The Journal, February 2, 2011. thejournal.com/articles/2011/02/02/the-backwards-class.aspx.

CHAPTER 3

Boaler, Joan and Lang Chen. "Why Kids Should Use Their Fingers in Math Class." The Atlantic. April 13, 2016. https://www.theatlantic.com/education/archive/2016/04/why-kids-should-use-their-fingers-in-math-class/478053.

Peyser, Marc. "Kids Who Count with Their Fingers Are Smarter." Reader's Digest. March 13, 2017. rd.com/health/wellness/counting-with-fingers.

Acknowledgments

First and foremost, I have to thank my family. Mom, you are my inspiration. You sparked my interest and talent in math and taught me from an early age what great teaching is all about. You are an incredibly positive force in my life, and I have nobody to thank more than you. Dad, everyone knows that I am my father's daughter. I have you to thank for my work ethic and stamina. You have pushed me to become the very best version of myself and taught me what true, selfless kindness looks like. Thank you for shaping me into the person I have become. And to my sister: Thank you for encouraging me through your own outgoing example to journey outside my comfort zone. You have taught me so much about being a strong, confident, daring woman.

Michael Summers, I first happened upon your artwork when I was at a conference in San Diego. I walked past a random art gallery, and your artwork, Flight of Fantasy, stopped me in my tracks. That bringing of a little "color back into our lives by working to achieve something positive and beautiful in the world" resonated so strongly with me. Having your artwork on my cover is a true dream come true! I still cannot believe your kindness in helping design my cover art, purely out of the goodness of your heart.

Dr. Charlene Kannankeril, thank you for your individualized approach to medicine and treatment. Thank you for listening deeply, thank you for understanding, thank you for identifying and making me aware of my personal needs, and thank you for helping me heal. It has been a long road and a bumpy journey. I'm not sure I would have made it out without you.

I'd like to thank all my colleagues at Bullis. I have learned an incredible amount and have received nothing but the most amazing support to innovate and push the boundaries of the traditional classroom. My head of school, Jerry Boarman, you have been behind me from day one, and I am thankful for your innovative vision for making tech integration an integral part of what we do here at Bullis. I would not be where I am today without my technology director, Jamie Dickie. I remember back in 2010, when you took me to my first Building Learning Communities (BLC) conference. The last session we went to was on the top ten educators to follow on Twitter. And you told me, "You're going to be up there one day, on that list and presenting." I looked at you thinking, *Yeah, right!* Jamie, you have been a constant, guiding force in my growth. My principal, Bobby Pollicino, you have helped me become a leader. You are receptive and open to new ideas and genuinely interested in my opinion on how we can improve teaching and learning at Bullis. The work that I get to do with you has transformed the way I am able to impact the teachers I work with. My former principal, Andy Delinsky, you trusted me and provided such solid guidance, encouragement, and support. I'll always feel incredibly lucky to have had you to learn from early in my teaching career. Faith Darling, you are one of the most amazing, talented people I know. We all need that trusted colleague who we can go to for advice or to just air out what's on our mind. Not only are you that person, but you are also a genius in your vision and ability to guide, mentor, and coach those around you. Faith, I've learned so much from your kind, compassionate leadership style. And thank you for being my accountability buddy, springboard for ideas, and friend for all these years. Stefi Tonrey, you make me smile every day; you are my sunshine. Thank you, Stefi, for being such a kind, loving, caring friend. Lisa Vardi, you are full of bold ideas and constantly dare me to dream big. I'm dreaming big now, Lisa! Maureen Martin, I'm so thankful for the balance and moment of zen you bring to my day. Lisa Gray, you've known my "secret" longer than anybody at school. Thank you for gently guiding, never judging, and always listening with genuine interest. Mark Riffee, you are so thoughtful, and your attention to detail is incredible! You're a huge inspiration. And the hugest thank you for my headshot; your work will forever be in my first book. Marc Steren, your questions and guidance have allowed me to grow to new levels. Thank you for your confidence and advice. My college counseling office mates—Francesca Brant, Lynn Kittel, Valerie Miller, Jina Walker, and Phil Weisgold—what can I say, you all are just the best; there is no better office on campus to walk into on a daily basis. You all have become friends, and I feel so lucky to be surrounded by such a wonderful group of kind, generous people. Lynn, thank you for being such a solid sounding board and trusted colleague. Beth Crowley, though we just started working together, already you have helped me find ways to make my voice shine brighter and bigger. You make me even more excited about what's to come. Nathan Stanford, I'll always include you as a Bullis friend whether you're close or far. Nobody can match your curiosity and sense of wonder and play.

My other major thanks goes to Alan November and that first BLC conference I attended in 2010. Hands down, BLC is one of the best learning opportunities I've found. Alan, you are a true visionary, and your words have had tremendous impact on my teaching. You helped me reimagine my classroom and shift my mentality. Your simple question of "Who owns the learning?" has been instrumental in shaping my work and helping me understand how critical it was to get away from the front of the room and empower my students.

Jo Boaler, your research and message gave me the confidence and encouragement to write this book. Thank you for inspiring me to be brave enough to tell my story. Susan Cain, you not only taught me it is okay to be an introvert, but you also allowed me to bring practices into my classroom that I naturally was inclined to but hesitated to implement, for fear that it would not promote the level of collaboration that I "should" aim for. Don't get me wrong; I am a strong believer in building a community inside my classroom where conversations flow naturally and continuously. But there should be a time and space for quiet, individual thought when needed. And you allowed me to shift my classroom to provide this.

Dave McCollom and Rachael Parker at TechSmith, you were the first ones to help me share my flipped classroom with the world. Thank you for opening that window of opportunity. Doug Little at Wacom, thank you for helping me figure out how to bring a class set of Wacom tablets to my classroom. Once discovered, I could finally bring some crazy cool ideas to life!

Tom Murray, Chris Walsh, Rod Berger, Joe Mazza, Ramsey Musallam, you were the first people I contacted when I decided I wanted to get this book published; I thank you for being constant mentors and amazingly generous with your time. Tom, in particular, you have never been too busy to provide that nudge in the right direction and guidance that I've been looking for; I thank you so much.

Finally, my publisher, Dave and Shelley Burgess. You were excited about my story from day one. You were genuinely interested in having me share my whole journey, and I am forever thankful for your support and enthusiasm. My editor, Erin Casey and her team at My Writers' Connection, I cannot thank you enough. You've made my words more powerful and brought life to this entire project.

There are so many others I want to thank, but I will wrap this up by saying how grateful I am to be surrounded by such an amazing community of support.

More from

DAVE BURGESS
Consulting, Inc.

Since 2012, DBCI has been publishing books that inspire and equip educators to be their best. For more information on our DBCI titles or to purchase bulk orders for your school, district, or book study, visit **DaveBurgessConsulting.com/DBCIBooks**.

More from the Like a *PIRATE*™ Series

Teach Like a PIRATE by Dave Burgess

Explore Like a Pirate by Michael Matera

Learn Like a Pirate by Paul Solarz

Play Like a Pirate by Quinn Rollins

Run Like a Pirate by Adam Welcome

Lead Like a PIRATE™ Series

Lead Like a PIRATE by Shelley Burgess and Beth Houf

Balance Like a Pirate by Jessica Cabeen, Jessica Johnson, and Sarah Johnson

Lead with Culture by Jay Billy

Lead with Literacy by Mandy Ellis

Lead beyond Your Title by Nili Bartley

Leadership & School Culture

Culturize by Jimmy Casas

Escaping the School Leader's Dunk Tank by Rebecca Coda
  and Rick Jetter

The Innovator's Mindset by George Couros

Kids Deserve It! by Todd Nesloney and Adam Welcome

Let Them Speak! by Rebecca Coda and Rick Jetter

Start. Right. Now. by Todd Whitaker, Jeffrey Zoul, and
  Jimmy Casas

Stop. Right. Now. by Jimmy Casas and Jeffrey Zoul Jetter

The Limitless School by Abe Hege and Adam Dovico

The Pepper Effect by Sean Gaillard

The Principled Principal by Jeffrey Zoul and
  Anthony McConnell

The Secret Solution by Todd Whitaker, Sam Miller, and
  Ryan Donlan

They Call Me "Mr. De" by Frank DeAngelis

Unmapped Potential by Julie Hasson and Missy Lennard

Your School Rocks by Ryan McLane and Eric Lowe

Technology & Tools

50 Things You Can Do with Google Classroom by Alice Keeler
  and Libbi Miller

50 Things to Go Further with Google Classroom by Alice Keeler
  and Libbi Miller

140 Twitter Tips for Educators by Brad Currie, Billy Krakower,
  and Scott Rocco

Code Breaker by Brian Aspinall

Creatively Productive by Lisa Johnson

Google Apps for Littles by Christine Pinto and Alice Keeler

Master the Media by Julie Smith

Shake Up Learning by Kasey Bell

Social LEADia by Jennifer Casa-Todd

Teaching Math with Google Apps by Alice Keeler and
  Diana Herrington

Teaching Methods & Materials

All 4s and 5s by Andrew Sharos

Ditch That Homework by Matt Miller and Alice Keeler

Ditch That Textbook by Matt Miller

Educated by Design by Michael Cohen

The EduProtocol Field Guide by Marlena Hebern and
  Jon Corippo

Instant Relevance by Denis Sheeran

LAUNCH by John Spencer and A.J. Juliani

Make Learning MAGICAL by Tisha Richmond

Pure Genius by Don Wettrick

Shift This! by Joy Kirr

Spark Learning by Ramsey Musallam

Sparks in the Dark by Travis Crowder and Todd Nesloney

Table Talk Math by John Stevens

The Classroom Chef by John Stevens and Matt Vaudrey

The Wild Card by Hope and Wade King

The Writing on the Classroom Wall by Steve Wyborney

Inspiration, Professional Growth, & Personal Development

The Four O'Clock Faculty by Rich Czyz

Be REAL by Tara Martin

Be the One for Kids by Ryan Sheehy

The EduNinja Mindset by Jennifer Burdis

How Much Water Do We Have? by Pete and Kris Nunweiler

P Is for Pirate by Dave and Shelley Burgess

The Path to Serendipity by Allyson Apsey

Through the Lens of Serendipity by Allyson Apsey

Sanctuaries by Dan Tricarico

Shattering the Perfect Teacher Myth by Aaron Hogan

Stories from Webb by Todd Nesloney

Talk to Me by Kim Bearden

The Zen Teacher by Dan Tricarico

Children's Books

Dolphins in Trees by Aaron Polansky

The Princes of Serendip by Allyson Apsey

Bring the Power of Compassionate Technology to Your School

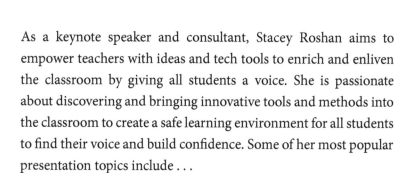

As a keynote speaker and consultant, Stacey Roshan aims to empower teachers with ideas and tech tools to enrich and enliven the classroom by giving all students a voice. She is passionate about discovering and bringing innovative tools and methods into the classroom to create a safe learning environment for all students to find their voice and build confidence. Some of her most popular presentation topics include . . .

- How to Use Technology to Strengthen Relationships, Ease Anxiety, and Empower All Students with a Voice
- Using Edtech to Personalize Learning
- Flipping the Classroom to Create Student-Centered Learning
- Shifting Educator and School Culture to Inspire Active Participation

Connect with Stacey Roshan
TechieMusings.com
@buddyxo
youtube.com/staceyroshan

About the Author

Stacey Roshan is the director of innovation and educational technology at Bullis School in Potomac, Maryland. She is passionate about discovering and bringing innovative tools into the classroom to create a safe learning environment for all students to find their voice and build confidence. Her work has been featured in major media outlets such as *USA Today*, *The Washington Post*, CNN and *PBS Newshour*. She has also been named Teacher of the Future by the National Association of Independent Schools. She earned a BA in economics at New York University and an MA in the subject at University of Virginia. In addition to teaching high school students to love and understand math, Stacey works closely with faculty and staff to design tech-infused lessons aimed at providing the optimal learning environment for all students. She frequently speaks at conferences and is a consultant and teacher ambassador to a number of edtech companies.

Lightning Source UK Ltd.
Milton Keynes UK
UKHW021532030920
369293UK00009B/1722